There's Something I Think You Should Know

A Youth Pastor's Last Words To His Students

Jon Morrison

authorHOUSE®

AuthorHouse™
1663 Liberty Drive
Bloomington, IN 47403
www.authorhouse.com
Phone: 1-800-839-8640

First published by AuthorHouse   6/26/2009

ISBN: 978-1-4389-7457-6 (e)
ISBN: 978-1-4389-7455-2 (sc)
ISBN: 978-1-4389-7456-9 (hc)

Printed in the United States of America
Bloomington, Indiana

This book is printed on acid-free paper.

To my family, friends, students and my Savior,
I wouldn't have been able to do anything without you.
This book is my gift to you.

Table of Contents

Foreword

My entire life, I have felt a disconnect between my generation and the ones before us. Music changes, technology evolves, and one-time lively youth settle down into their oft-stereotyped roles as adults. For those of us traversing the rough road known as adolescence, it often leaves us with the gaze of observers rather than the hand of mentors. It's an incredible blessing, then, to know a man who offers not only a hand, but his entire self, for the students he is passionate about guiding.

I first met Jon Morrison two years ago as my church's new youth pastor, in a time of great change in my life. While no single person or event can be given recognition for the growth I experienced, Jon was inarguably a catalyst, helping initiate a series of events that would provide greater experiences and a far more intimate knowledge of God than I ever would have expected.

Where some may focus on bowling trips and laser tag, Jon has inspired a passion for service, chivalry, legitimacy and outreach within our youth group. At the risk of discomfort, he has never failed to challenge us to embrace God's best for us, for followers to become leaders and boys to become men. To "dream big dreams", and follow them to whatever conclusion they reach.

In an age when the divide between teens and the generation before them seems to be ever-growing, I suggest we not take for granted the opportunity this is, to benefit from Jon's transparency, experiences and insight into the world we as graduates are about to step into; a world I imagine will be full of greater heights, harder lows, larger lessons and more to hope for than the one we've found ourselves in so far. Let's meet it head-on.

Matthew Newton, 17
Dr. Charles Best Secondary, Class of '09

Introduction

This spring I will attend my ten year high school reunion. In June of 1999 I walked across the platform graduating from Seycove Secondary School as just another face in the crowd. I recently looked at my pictures of that day and began to reminisce about all that has happened since then.

I thought about the kid in the picture. I thought about all the things that were going to happen in his life, all the lessons he was going to learn, about the successes he would enjoy, and the heartache and disappointment he would endure in the coming years. I thought about how great it would be to have the opportunity to take him out for lunch and tell him all about it. There's something I think he should know.

I would have offered some advice that would have helped him through those experiences. In hindsight, he needed some perspective on how to really enjoy the good times, and some wisdom on how to persevere through the difficult days.

This book has taken me these last 10 years to write. It is a result of the lessons I have learned and the discontent with the books that are out there on the market aimed at graduating students. Young people today come with built in Tupperware detectors — they can smell plastic a mile away. Most books for graduates are more plastic than a Beverly Hills cocktail party; the obvious solution was to write my own.

I do not want this to be another book in an already flooded market of Christian books written by white guys with an agenda. I couldn't help but write something that I thought would help my students on their journey ahead. Writing a book seemed to be the best way to communicate that.

Jesus said, "To whom much has been given, much will be expected." I have been blessed with the ability to write and create, and it is a pleasure to share it with those that read these pages. I am forever grateful for the support I have received from people who have invested so much of themselves into my life. To my many role models, mentors, pastors, friends and teachers who saw something inside this punk kid worth pouring a good portion of their time and prayers into, I say thank you. And it hasn't just been people. I have had many dollars invested in my education at Ambrose University College, various retreats, conferences and the many books that I have been given over the years — all of which I have devoured.

I have been given much, and now I pray that I will be able to return a portion of that which has been lavishly invested into me.

Allow Me To Introduce... Myself

I am grateful to be the son of two very loving and supportive parents. They taught me that I could be anything or do anything that I wanted in life. They each made tremendous sacrifices throughout my childhood to help me become all God intended me to be. They have been there each step of the way in this marathon race of life, handing me water bottles at the thirstiest of times.

As I come from a rich Christian heritage, my mom and grandma taught me about Jesus and that nothing is impossible when you have devoted your life to Him. It was my mom who taught me how to dream as well as how to pick myself up when I saw my dreams die.

My dream for the majority of my life was to be an NHL goaltender. Like most Canadian kids, I wanted nothing more in life than to hoist Lord Stanley's Cup above my head and make the famous skate around the ice. I was willing to do whatever it took to get to that point: spending long hours all year round on the ice, going to the gym and doing my best to avoid girls. Girls were off limits. They were weapons of mass distraction in the battle to get to the NHL. In my late teens I was given the opportunity to play Junior hockey and the next step was earning a hockey scholarship to some big US school. I watched as, one-by-one, my closest friends were signed to play hockey for big NCAA schools and wondered when my turn would come. My story is different from their stories, however. After playing my last game of the season at the age of twenty, God began changing my heart as to what my future could look like. I began to realize that there was something else out there for me other than struggling to make a career in hockey. God made it clear that, as a Christian, my life's ambition was not to make myself famous, but to live in a way that made His name famous. I wasn't to follow my dreams for my life but to follow His dream for me.

At a youth conference I snuck into one spring, I sensed God wanted me to start pouring my time, talent and energy into His purpose for my life rather than chasing my own feeble plans. He wanted to use me as a part of his transforming work in the lives of young people. I immediately lost all excitement in getting hit with high speed rubber pucks and instead committed to letting Jesus do all the saving from that point on.

My whole life has been radically changed since that youth conference. I went home and sold my goalie equipment to pay for a great experience at Bible School. After graduating, I found work as a youth pastor where I now get a front row seat to witness God's powerful work in the transformation of young lives. Watching Jesus get a hold of a teenager's life is like winning a Stanley Cup but much better. The Stanley Cup will one day turn to rust but peoples' lives last for eternity.

It's all about perspective.

There is nothing I would rather do in the world than what I do now. Chasing down my dream for my life resulted in nothing but frustration, anger, disappointment, tears and pain. Though I still experience those things, I experience them knowing that I am doing exactly what I was created to do. I realize that I am one of the fortunate few that can make such a claim.

"All I Ever Wanted" is my life's story. I think you will understand why:

Growing up I was often frustrated that my Dad didn't give me everything I wanted. No matter what I asked for, it seemed like he always had a better idea for me. It got annoying sometimes.

For example, there was the time we were in the garage and I was having trouble putting a box away.

"I want to be the strongest man in the world one day, Dad," I told him. "Then I won't need anyone's help. Ever."

"True strength comes when you are weakest, my son. Never be afraid to ask for help."

I remember playing catch in the yard and asking Dad if he could teach me to play so well that I would never drop a ball.

He said that balls needed to be dropped so that you would always remember to laugh at yourself.

We were fixing the truck one night and I asked Dad if he could make sure that nothing ever went wrong with my life.

He said that things need to go wrong because that's how we grow. As you grow, you can help other people who need to grow too.

I asked my Dad if I could be a powerful king one day and have lots of servants who would give me everything I wanted right when I wanted them.

He told me that kind of power would ruin my life. He said that the best people in the world are not those who seek to be served but those who seek to serve.

One night as I was going to bed, I asked my Dad to tell me what tomorrow would be like.

He said that I wouldn't want to know what tomorrow would hold even if he could tell me. He said the most fun is discovering each day as it comes.

I asked Dad if I could be popular — the most famous person in the entire world. I asked if I could win over the masses with empty promises and simple rhetoric like "Yes We Can!"

He said that people were not made for that kind of popularity. He said fame makes people crazy.

As I grew up I dreamed about shiny new cars. Dad said happiness does not come from a machine.

I asked Dad to buy me a big, new house.

He said it's best to build a mansion in heaven.

I asked Dad for money to buy everything I ever wanted.

He told me how the richest people he knew were all poor.

Now that I think about it, he's right.

Looking back I see that all that I thought I wanted, I didn't really need. I got nothing that I asked for but everything I hoped for.

I, among all men, am the most blessed.

That story is my testimony. It is a story about what God has done in my life — His love, His work, His grace, His mercy and His faithfulness. I have experienced all of those things and much more. My life is a testimony to the grace of my Lord, Jesus Christ. Without Him I would be nothing.

About This Book

If you want to write a book, you don't have to be a superhero, an intellectual, a professional athlete or a celebrity of any sort. You just have to do it; that means being willing to sit in random places with a laptop as your only companion and spending seemingly countless hours just typing and typing.

In the process of writing, I discovered that everyone, in fact, is secretly writing a book of their own. Few ever sit down to write it out physically but that doesn't mean the dream is not still there. So take my advice and go write yours…after you're done with mine of course. It would be foolish to stop now. We've come so far already.

If you are a recent graduate, you have many lessons to learn in the coming years. I hope that this book will offer you a few insights and tips to help you make the learning curve a little less steep and much more enjoyable. If you are not graduating, feel free to read on. There should be something you need to know as well. My hope is that, whoever or wherever you are, going through these next chapters will not be unlike the puberty experience — awkward at times and challenging at others — in the end, you're glad you went through it.

You will find chapters on some of the issues I dealt with as a young adult. There is stuff like how to deal with doubt, what Christians really believe about hell, the cross and going to heaven. How to answer the dreaded "What are you going to do after school?" question, and how to get the most out of your short time on earth. We will also look at what to do when your life falls apart which may or may not be closely connected with the how to deal with relationships and the dating chapter.

I would encourage you to take time at the end of each chapter to reflect on what you have read. I had to cram a lot into each section and it would be a shame to miss out because you rushed through it.

Pulling off a feat such as writing a book is a team effort. Being one who is prone to overlook details, I often go about my day with my fly left down and e-brake on my car left up. Given such tendencies, it was important to surround myself with some great people who provided support in the whole editing process. I would like to take a second to thank some of the people who helped me get this book out in your hands. These heroes of mine are Rosalyn Vath, Jeremy Kyle, Patti Morrison and Christina Basri. For your tireless help and many suggestions, thank you. To Coquitlam Alliance Church, for giving a young punk his first shot in the big leagues, thank you. I would also like to thank my youth staff and my amazing students. You guys are the greatest and you make it fun to show up for work each day. Thanks to you for reading this. By taking the time to read this book, you have made these hours of studying, wrestling, living, observing, typing and editing all worthwhile. I did it all for you because...

There's something I think you should know.

Dealing With Doubt

When A Pastor Has A Hard Time Believing In God

"I find your lack of faith…disturbing."
–Darth Vader.

I know I'm a pastor so I'm not supposed to say this but I will let you in on one of my struggles — I sometimes doubt if God is real or not. I wonder why, if He is really out there, why He doesn't show up when I ask Him to or why He doesn't do the things I tell Him to do. That's just my life. How about all the problems around the world? How about all the people who openly deny Him and get away with it. Sometimes all of those things add up at once and I wonder if this Christianity thing is just something that I've been brainwashed into believing and that someone, somewhere is making a lot of money because of all the billions of Christian chumps around the world who are as naive as I am...

I'm a pastor, I know — it's a little weird that I think this way.

The strangest thing happens on some mornings. I wake up and I don't want to believe in God anymore. Is it that I don't *want* to believe in Him or just that I simply don't believe in Him anymore? It's probably both. My problems are affected by my

1

emotions and they get in the way of what I know to be fact. Sometimes I let those emotional doubts run wild in my mind which leaves the facts frantically chasing after them.

Mornings like these are a big problem for me. There's a lot on the line when it comes to God and I let me tell you. You see, I work at a church. In fact, I'm a leader of a large ministry at a church. If you were an atheist, you might get away with being a church janitor or an elder at such a holy institution, but if you are a pastor who is in charge of praying at mealtimes, preaching and trying to lead people into a closer relationship with God, you'd better believe in God. It's kind of a given.

On these faith-deprived mornings, I have to take the time to get my beliefs straight before I go to work. So as I sit at the breakfast table, I pour my Cheerios, and recite what I believe as a Christian and why I believe it. I have done this often and each time I wrestle with my doubts about God and the Christian faith, I emerge more confident in what I believe, or rather Who I believe in.

I started the book with this chapter because there is no doubt in my mind (pun intended) that you will share a similar experience with doubts about God as you venture into the rest of your life. You may go to college and come face-to-face with the new breed of militant atheists who seek to destroy theism (a belief in God) in society, especially the Christian faith. Maybe you are reading this and you do not believe in God at all. Maybe today you are somewhere in between You have a strong suspicion that something or Someone is out there; you just don't know who they are.

I think I know what you are going through. It is not uncommon to wrestle with the big question at some point in life, "Does God really exist?" I do not have all the answers but I do have experience dealing with this question in my own journey. Below I will explain how I deal with doubt over a bowl of cereal on those faithless mornings.

First, here are some common roadblocks that keep people from walking the path to experiencing the true Creator God.

1. Militant Atheism

There is a lot of money to be made in trying to prove God is not real. I'm sure by now you have seen either a movie, documentary, read a book or watched some sort of Youtube video revealing a "new discovery" that has proved Christianity false or found the missing link to atheistic evolution. One day you could be watching the news and find out someone has discovered that Jesus in fact had three wives — two of whom were aliens and one a mermaid.

The arguments are always convincing on the surface and their presenters seem charming enough to believe. But dig only a little and you will soon find that their arguments are poorly researched and lack integrity. For examples of this, one needs to do very little research on all the holes with Dan Brown's *Da Vinci Code* argument, *Zeitgeist* or James Cameron's work *The Jesus Family Tomb*.

Though atheists work hard at trying to disprove God and will piggyback off media support, I have yet to find a compelling and trustworthy argument that urges me to ditch my faith in God. That does not stop them from producing new material and I do not blame them. They're great businessmen.

2. Church History

I have empathy for people who have studied church history and have concluded that if this is the way God's people behave, they want nothing to do with God or His church. There are some ugly chapters in the story of the Christian Church. Many terrible things were done in the name of Jesus that have made that name repulsive to its victims and those who have studied history. I am embarrassed by some of these shameful and

3

inexcusable acts though I am reminded that Jesus himself warned that there would be punishment for anyone who gets in the way of a person's belief in God[1]. Jesus also said that many would come in His name who knew nothing about truly following Him. He warned us that evildoers would show up wearing our jersey but really playing for the wrong team.

It's not just church history that can cause a lot of damage to faith in Jesus. I hate late night white haired preachers as well. I do not know how these guys keep getting funded to spill their garbage all over the air. I know about the monetary fraud, the sex scandals and the hypocrisy that is prevalent in the church. It grieves me and I believe it grieves God too — especially if it is keeping you from believing in Him.

The alternatives to "organized religion" in recent years have proved just as bleak. The past century has been the bloodiest in history and, arguably, the most secular. One of the most interesting and often overlooked paradoxes in the history of humanity is that the most violent and intolerant acts have been committed by those who were trying to rid us of violent and intolerable acts[2]. The communist regimes of Russia, China and Cambodia, for example, all rejected organized religion or any belief in God and produced some of the most horrific large-scale massacres of their own people. Hitler and the Nazis traded the preciousness of divine-given human dignity for horrific acts motivated by their belief that they were a superior race and must rule the world and that lesser beings should be done away with. We know the result of that. This is why I do not buy into the agenda of those who claim that religion is responsible for all the violence of history; it's just not true.

---

[1] See Jesus' warning in Matthew 18:5-6
[2] Inspired by McGrath, Alistair. *The Dawkins Delusion? Atheist Fundamentalism and the Denial Of The Divine* (Inter-Varsity Press, 2007), p.81.

3. Bad Experiences With The Church

Sometimes I want to run away from Christianity because Christians can drive me nuts. A lot of people, myself included, will say something silly like, "I cannot believe in God because I've been hurt by the church." I always visualize in my head just how people actually get hurt from a church. Do they run into a door, have a beam fall on their head, burn their tongue with scalding church coffee? How exactly does this happen? Usually what they mean is that they have had an issue with a person or group of people – people who represent Christians to them – and that those people have done them harm. In such a case, it would be unwise to use the hurt caused by a broken relationship as a proof against the existence of God. Rather than run away from God because one is hurting, the best idea would be to run to Him to find help and healing. Besides, if you did manage to eventually reconcile with the person(s) that hurt you, would that mean that God now existed?

I will quote C.S. Lewis to wrap up this point quite well.

> If what you want is an argument against Christianity... you can easily find some stupid and unsatisfactory Christian and say...'So there's your boasted new man! Give me the old kind.' But if once you have begun to see that Christianity is on other grounds probable, you will know in your heart that this is only evading the issue. What can you know of other people's souls — of their temptations, their opportunities, their struggles? One soul in the whole creation you do know: and it is the only one whose fate is placed in your hands. If there is a God, you are, in a sense, alone with Him. You cannot put Him off with speculations about your next-door neighbours or memories of what you read in books. What will all that chatter and hearsay count when the anesthetic fog we call 'nature' or 'the real world' fades away and the Divine

Presence in which you have always stood becomes palpable, immediate, and unavoidable?[3]"

What C.S. Lewis is saying is that in every case with all humans, be they Christian, atheist, pastor, engineer or barista, it is not enough for you to hide behind excuses about *other people* for why *you* did not believe in God. Eventually we will each stand before our Creator and all our excuses, however convincing, will not matter anymore. It will be hard to stand in front of the Living God and explain to Him why you think He does not exist.

A Sympathetic Word About Doubt

I don't think that there is anything wrong with doubt as long as it is a doubt that is actively seeking to get answers. There are many people in the Bible who doubted God and even wrestled with Him to get help for their questions. When Jesus walked on the earth, people often doubted Him and questioned whether or not He was all that He said He was. His own disciples, who spent three years hanging out with Him everyday, were amongst the most skeptical. C'mon now guys, you're hanging out with God! He's right there healing sick people, feeding thousands with a baguette and a couple fish, walking on water, raising people from the dead. How much more evidence do you need? There is a funny verse right at the end of Matthew's gospel that should be comfort to the modern day skeptic. Jesus had been publicly crucified on the cross and three days later He shows up again to His disciples and a bunch of others. The risen Jesus is standing there in front of them giving a few last words of instruction and probably encouraging them to pick their jaws up off the ground. There is Jesus — the one they've been hanging out with all these years — the one they saw arrested, whipped, crucified and then buried. Now He's standing there in front of them again. And this is what Matthew says happened in that unprecedented and miraculous moment:

---

[3] Lewis, C.S., *Mere Christianity* (Macmillan, 1965), p.168.

6

"When they saw him, they worshiped him." You bet they did. They didn't all worship though. Verse 17 goes on to say, "but some doubted." Doubted? Really?

I do not feel so bad about doubting God anymore and neither should you. I mean we are over two thousand years removed since Jesus walked on Middle Eastern sand. We are living in a world of laptops, cell phones, flat screen TVs, and flying cars (well not at the immediate time of writing but if you ever watched the end-times cartoon "The Jetsons," you know it's going to happen any day now). In today's modern age I can understand why we could have legitimate doubts about believing in a God who floods the earth, separates rivers, has Jonah spend a couple nights in Hotel De Whale, makes a blind man see using spit and mud, and claims to be coming back again any day. It would take faith to believe God did and still does those kinds of things.

The Journey Back To Faith

Here are some of my reasons for why I believe it is more rational to believe in God than to deny His existence. Again remember, I am a pastor and not a scientist so this is simply my journey from doubt to faith. I would point you to brilliant men like Ravi Zacharias, Lee Strobel, Tim Keller for more in depth info.

I should probably state that there is no way to prove God's existence. At no point can we put a substance in a test tube, label it "God" and then conduct the "Does God exist?" experiment over and over. If we could do that with God, He wouldn't be God, the Creator of humanity; it would be more like humanity, the creator of God.

I like Tim Keller's view on finding "proofs" to prove the existence of God[4]. He argues that there are none. On every point I will make there is a rational escape route out of it. Instead of finding definitive proofs, Keller argues that we are to look instead for clues that point to the existence of God or what has also been called, "divine fingerprints" showing us that He is there. These are the God-clues that have helped me the most.

1. Purpose

Where did everything come from? If not God, then what? What are the alternatives to a belief in a higher power? Let's get it straight that science has nothing to say about origins — as in where things come from. The theory of evolution is about how things develop and adapt, not how they got started. The role of the scientist is to say, "On this day I put this in a tube and when I mixed it with this substance, this was the outcome." When you start to talk about beginnings you are leaving the boundaries of science and entering the arena of the philosopher. When you're talking about a time when no one was there, you are left to speculation and faith. Christians and scientists tell faith stories when talking about how the earth was formed. The question then is, whose faith story is right?

The atheists' faith story is that billions of years ago a series of highly improbable occurrences happened. Non-living elements came together and in a several billion year process we have the creation of life. This set off other multi billion year processes involving random mutations that brought us the introduction of simple organisms, plants, fish, birds, animals and then sometime between then and now, you arrived.

I find this faith story quite depressing. If we came from a bunch of cosmic accidents with no real direction, how do you find any meaning in life? If I came from nowhere and am bound for

---

[4]   See Keller, Tim. *The Reason For God.* (Penguin Group, 2008), p. 128.

nowhere, the only question I am left to ask is whether or not suicide matters; is life worth living? Is my time on earth really worth anything? Without an answer that starts with a Creator, life is bleak. It's hopeless. As I said, it's really depressing.

In the faith story about the God of the Bible I find a reference point for a beginning which is a step in a more reasonable direction. Our life experience shows us you never get something from nothing. In the Bible, God is that Something that creates everything and that makes sense.

I'm ok with the big bang theory if that is what science deems most probable (but I'm still accepting applications for other theories at the time of writing). A trusted scientist, Stephen Hawking has said, "Almost everyone now believes that the universe, and time itself, had a beginning at the Big Bang.[5]" A big bang neither proves nor disproves the existence of God, it only suggests a beginning coming from somewhere. At this point in historical scientific discovery, I'm totally fine with that.

Let's use this theory and trace it back to its logical beginning. To argue that this "Big Bang" happened all by itself without any help is to treat this bang unlike any bang you have experienced before. If you are inside your house and hear a bang, you are going to start asking questions like "What happened? Did someone light a firecracker, shoot a gun, did a bomb go off? How did that bang start? Where did that particular bang come from?" This is our reason working with our experience from the law of contingents that says that something always has a cause outside of itself. The farmer bought some seeds and planted them; that caused some beans to grow, which caused him to put them in a can, which caused your mom to cook them, which caused some gas, which caused you to leave the room, which got you started on your homework... everything is contingent

---

5   Hawking, Stephen and Penrose, Robert. *The Nature of Time and Space* (Princeton University Press, 1996) p.20

on everything else. It is also known as the law of cause and effect.

In the Bible, God is the self-existent cause who initiates everything. He is the One in whom all contingents find their origin. God exists outside of time and is the only one who could get the proverbial ball rolling. If you're having a hard time grasping a being that exists outside of time, I can hardly blame you. Time is all we know — we are confined to it as a limitation of being human. As I read about the God of the Bible, I'm willing to admit that he's bigger than me and can figure stuff out that I don't understand at all.

Other ancient mythological creation stories start with a chaotic battle in the heavens and, out of violence and strife, the material world is created. The Bible is different. The biblical story of creation is a Hebrew poem revealing a deeply relational and loving Trinitarian God who creates a world to share love and relationship with His new creation. I don't know how He pulled the whole thing off — I wasn't there and neither was anyone else, but I do believe God did it. He did it with a plan in mind for the completed work of His hands. He did it with purpose and beauty, and wherever I travel, I admire the fine job God did. Without God, I can thank no one — just billions of years of randomness.

Thinking about the natural beauty and order of the world, I am lead to my next clue as I take a few more bites of Cheerios and realize that a beautiful design must come from a very skilled Designer.

2. Design

Have you ever looked at a painting and wondered who was responsible for such a masterpiece? Ever listened to a song and wondered who wrote it? We see beautiful things and naturally want to give people credit for creating them. It really should not be any different with God. This world is beautiful. He made it that way.

I look around and realize there is simply too much beauty and design for all of this to be a pointless coincidence. Having had the privilege to travel the world, I have seen God's work as a master creator everywhere I go: a beautiful beach in Australia, a sunset in the Prairies, surfing the waves in Costa Rica, the red dirt of Africa, driving through the Rocky Mountains. I love going for a hike in the summer through rivers and valleys or standing at the top of a snowy mountain in winter overlooking the city or endless backcountry.

While discussing intricate design, how about the specimen that is you, a human being? People are amazing. One time I went on a date to a science exhibit called *Bodyworks*, a display where they take dead people and turn them into plastic. It's not the most romantic venue but it was fascinating to see what is going on inside of our bodies all the time. Breathing, eating, sleeping — there's a lot going on in there. I learned how the skeleton works with the muscular system in connection with the nervous system with our hearts and our brains. The whole thing is connected and in some way it all comes together and makes you. It's unbelievable but it is very believable with a creative designer like God!

The more I hear musicians talk about the complexities of musical theory, the more it points me to God as well. What is it about the combination of a guitar, piano, and vocalist working in harmony that is so much more soothing to hear than a jackhammer, crow and alarm clock singing together in unison?

There are many other gifts of design God gave us — food being one of them. God could have made steak taste like cardboard and fruit like grass. We did not need to see in colour. Black and white would have been just fine to operate day to day. But God created it as a gift to us and it would be foolish not to thank Him for it[6].

Nature, people, music, food, colours; these experiences point me away from the accidental chaos of the atheistic worldview to the creative design of a very talented and detail-oriented God. To me, that kind of beauty cannot be the product of billions of chaotic coincidences — it has to be God.

That's how design affects me personally. But what about the other kinds of information that we take for granted? Francis Crick, the geneticist who discovered DNA, noted that in each human cell there is enough information to go back and forth from earth to sun several times. How do you get information without something programming that information in[7]? Your body is full of information, constantly checking back to your DNA, the body's blueprints, to rebuild itself.

There are other types of design as well that both fascinate me and serve as clues pointing me to my Creator. Like the fact that the summer sun is just far enough away that it doesn't burn us all up. The moon is the perfect distance from the earth to create the tides to surf on while also mixing the ocean's currents to prevent us all from freezing to death. The gravitational pull from the sun and moon gives the earth a perfect 23.5 degree tilt on its axis which enables us to enjoy the seasons. Due to the precise pull of both sun and moon we can have snowboarding in winter and wakeboarding in summer. It also provides a temperate climate on earth that sustains life. I'm pretty sure the latter is more important than the former but who's to say that breathing is more important than shredding through freshly fallen powder?

Scientists say that on our earth there are at least fifteen constants like this that enable us to experience life as we know it. Things

---

[6]   Psalm 14:1
[7]   Taken from a Rob Bell talk *Everything Is Spiritual*. (Zondervan, 2006)

like gravity, the proper heat levels from the sun, nuclear forces, hydrogen levels, etc. They are part of an argument for God known as the "fine tuning" argument. Picture a set of finely adjusted dials, all independent and yet fully dependent on one another to sustain life on earth. You move one of those dials even slightly and we are either burnt toast, frozen ice cubes or suffocated to death.

Scientist Francis Collins states it well,

> "When you look from the perspective of a scientist at the universe, it looks as if it knew we were coming… if any one of those (15) constants was off by even one part in a million, or in some cases, by one part in a million million, the universe could not have actually come to the point where we see it. Matter would not have been able to coalesce, there would have been no galaxy, stars, planets or people[8]."

I look at the design of the world and my reasoning alone cannot conclude that these constants are a result of random chance accidents. Collins was right; it seems that something or Someone set this place up for me to experience life on earth. I think of the complexity of a well-designed creation and am compelled to echo the words of the Psalmist, "When I consider the heavens, the work of your fingers, the moon and the stars which you have set in place, what is man that you are mindful of him?[9]"

3. Morality

If that is not convincing enough, there is another clue I use that assists the rebuilding of my faith from doubt. In the first three chapters of Mere Christianity, C.S. Lewis lays out a step-by-

---

[8]   Francis Collins. In an interview with Salon.com, *(www.salon. com/books/int/2006/08/07/collins/index2.html)* last accessed March 9, 2007.
[9]   Psalm 8:3

step explanation for how morality, the belief that some things are right and others are wrong, must be connected to a belief in God. To Lewis (and to common sense), you can't have a moral law without a moral Lawgiver.

If you do not have God as a Lawgiver, anything goes. If our origins are just a bunch of accidental mutations that started from a freak explosion of gases, what is stopping us from starving the poor, nuking a country or committing genocide on a race we don't particularly like? I see no explanation for "right behavior" — it's just your opinion versus mine. To anyone who disagrees with me while trying to appeal to any sort of third party standard, I only have to answer with a common response among 8 year olds, "Says Who?" No matter what judicial, governmental, or religious organizations may say, if I came from primordial cosmic soup, I can do whatever the heck I want. If any disagree with me, "Says who?"

But of course, I cannot do whatever I want. I am bound by conscience. When I act cowardly, lie, cheat, lust or steal, I know I have done something wrong. There is a conviction and my conscience holds me to a standard that I did not create and do not live up to. There is a moral law inside of me which I can either submit to or suppress. If you do not believe this, you are in serious denial. What stops you from stealing gas when you fill up your car? You know it is wrong. What stops you from killing the person you don't like? You know it's wrong. Why do we credit a soldier for acts of bravery? It's because we know that bravery is right and cowardice is wrong. That sense of right and wrong is the moral law God put inside each one of us.

But just who is this God?

4. The Bible

It is when you grasp the fact that there is a law, and that you and I break it all the time that Christianity starts to make the most sense. When you realize you are a lawbreaker by nature, the Christian message starts to look very appealing. C.S. Lewis writes of this experience,

> "When you know you are sick, you will listen to the doctor. When you have realized your position is nearly desperate you will begin to understand what the Christians are talking about. They offer an explanation of how we got into our present state of both hating goodness and loving it. They offer an explanation of how God can be this impersonal mind at the back of the Moral Law and yet also a Person[10]."

The Bible, the best selling book of all time, has come under intense scrutiny more than any other book in history. No matter what comes out in the news, whatever "new discoveries" are revealed, no matter what any guy with an Ivy League degree tells reporters on CNN, the Word of God will stand forever. The Bible says of itself, "The grass withers and the flowers fall, but the word of God stands forever[11]." That is a promise God gave Isaiah, now proven true with time. The Bible is the story of the greatest revolutionary and the focal point of history — the man who was called Jesus.

5. Jesus

There is no one like Him. Jesus of Nazareth is the most influential man that ever walked upon this earth. He spoke a radical, revolutionary message, so out of the box that it got Him killed. Jesus taught about how different things are in God's kingdom than how we do things on earth. He said that those who humble themselves would be honored, that the last will be first, and that giving is better than receiving. Jesus taught us how a man should not seek to *be* served but *to* serve, and

---

[10]   Lewis, C.S. *Mere Christianity*. (Fontana Books, 1942). P. 37-38.

[11]   Isaiah 40:8

that the secret to gaining your life is through losing it. A car runs best when fuelled by gasoline and a blender only runs with electricity. In the same way Jesus knew that human being runs best on His words. Without them, we break down. In my 27 years of living thus far, it is the people who truly live by Jesus' teachings who, as far as being human goes, "get it." Those who follow Jesus discover that He really does give "life to the full[12]." They discover the narrow road that leads to true life when they live their lives for others, take brave and bold stands for justice, and help the weak, poor and needy.

In Philip Yancey's book, *The Jesus I Never Knew*[13], Yancey contrasts his experiences as a journalist interviewing society's brightest "stars" with our much lesser known "servants." Spending years with our celebrities who dominate the media, are admired and imitated for the clothes they wear, the places they go, the parties they attend and even the toothpaste they use, Yancey observed that this group of people are characterized as

> "...miserable a group of people as I have ever met. Most have troubled or broken marriages. Nearly all are incurably dependent on psychotherapy. In heavy irony, these larger than life heroes seem tormented by self doubt."

On the other side of the popularity contest are the people that you will never hear about in the news: the doctors who work with leprosy patients in India, the faithful servants who have given their lives to working with the homeless in every city around the world, the nurses helping HIV patients in Africa, relief workers in Indonesia, New Orleans, Sudan, Rwanda, Darfur. Yancey has hung out with a bunch of these types as well. He notes,

---

[12] John 10:10
[13] Yancey, Phillip. *The Jesus I Never Knew,* (Zondervan, 1995) Pages 117-118.

"I was prepared to honor and admire these servants, to hold them up as inspiring examples. I was not prepared to envy them. Yet as I now reflect on the two groups side by side, stars and servants, the servants clearly emerge as the favored ones. Without question I would rather spend time among the servants... they possess qualities of depth and richness and even joy that I have not found elsewhere... in the process of losing their lives they find them[14]."

There is something about this Jesus and all He stood for that makes sense to me. It is certainly better than any of the celebrity nonsense we see in our culture today. For this reason, Christ is honored in history as a great teacher, a title He was often given though never asked for.

Jesus claimed not to be a teacher but to be God. Your response to such a claim can be twofold: He was either telling the truth or He was a wing nut. His mission, as God, was to die as a substitutionary sacrifice for humanity's sin, "to give his life as a ransom for many[15]." His death on the cross was the turning point in history as we see God punishing Himself in our place. Jesus died and then, to the shock of his followers and the entire world, He rose again from the dead. No one in those days ever expected anyone to actually rise from the dead but there was Jesus, three days later, alive and hanging out.

I am amazed when I think that He did all that for me. Not just me of course but I will be forever grateful that Christ was willing to humbly take on human form, and to suffer a horrendous and shameful death in order to pay the consequence of my sin. The Romans 5:8 declaration that "while we were still sinners, Christ died for us" takes on greater meaning the more I realize that there is literally nothing in me that seeks after God on my own, that believes in His existence all the time and that deserves the

---

[14] Ibid, page 118.
[15] Matthew 20:28

kind of grace Christ has shown me. It is truly, as Romans 2:4 states, "God's kindness leads you towards repentance."' When I realize all that Jesus has done for me, I cannot help but run towards Him and do whatever He would ask of me.

The longer I follow Jesus, the more convinced I am that He really is all he says He is. If there is a God, I believe there is no better representation of Divinity than what I find in Jesus Christ.

Faith Is Restored And It's Time For Work!

Today I believe that life has meaning and is worth living. I believe in love, beauty, and design and I know that this whole thing is not one big multi billion year old accident. I believe in right and wrong, that humans have intrinsic dignity and that justice should be served for those who violate it. To believe in all these things and yet fail to acknowledge the One who is responsible for it all would be to live a lie. To continue to deny God's existence after all this would not be due to a lack of evidence on His part, but the suppression of this evidence on my part.

By sitting and contemplating all these things, my faith in the God I serve feels strong again. I feel ready to go out and take on a new day serving Him as a pastor at my church. If you share these struggles with me, I hope this chapter has led you back to choose faith as well.

Look at that. All this thinking has made me late! I have to get to work.

Embracing The Journey

Seizing The Day

"Every man dies. Not every man really lives."
-William Wallace, Braveheart

I remember the day I realized my thinking needed to change before my whole life passed before my eyes.

When I was a kid, "getting big" was the goal of life. When you are older, life just seemed perfect. You don't have to do chores, you could drive a car, go on a plane, and drink coffee! My mom thought caffeine was the gateway drug to cocaine. I was never allowed to let caffeine touch my lips until I had moved out and formally cut the apron strings that bound us. Now that I'm older, I realize that I do not have any problems with coffee at all — I only have problems *without* coffee!

It wasn't just about being able to drink coffee. Grown-ups had so much freedom — they could do whatever they wanted to and could stay up to watch Letterman! Now that I am one, I see that being a grown-up is not what I imagined. Life did not work out as I thought it would. At the time of writing, I do not own a flying car, live in a gold house or work as a video game tester. For so many years all I wanted was to be a grown-up but now that I am a "grown-up," I wouldn't mind going back to being a kid again. I would love to have all my meat cut up for me, have someone pay all my bills and make it mandatory to set aside some time every day for napping.

During my hockey days, it was the same struggle. I held a misconceived belief that things would always get better as soon as I got one league higher. In minor hockey I wanted to play junior B; in junior B, I wanted to play junior A; in junior A, I wanted to play college hockey.

One day I realized that maybe things would never get better, maybe it was my attitude that needed to change and not the league I was in. It is scary to think that I let so much of this prime time of my life pass having never lived a single day of it. It is also scary to think that some people not only go through a few years like this, but their entire lives! Have you caught yourself with this kind of thinking yet?

Things will be better as soon as I graduate.

I will be much happier once I'm in university.

Or once I get my degree.

Or when I get into the right career.

Or once I get married.

Or when we have kids.

Or once I retire.

Things will be better once I'm dead.

When does it end? The end starts with today.

Seize it.

It's what they call "Carpe Diem."

Seize The Day, It's All You Have Right Now

In the 1989 film, *Dead Poets Society*, Robin Williams plays an inspiring teacher named Mr. Keating who encourages freethinking to a class of otherwise bored boarding school students. In the first English class of the new school year, Mr. Keating takes his students outside the class into a hallway to stare at a bunch of pictures of students from past years. As the students stare into the faces of their predecessors, Keating begins to teach his famous lesson,

> "They're not that different from you, are they? Same haircuts. Full of hormones, just like you. Invincible, just like how you feel. The world is their oyster. They believe they're destined for great things, just like many of you, their eyes are full of hope, just like you. Did they wait until it was too late to make from their lives even one iota of what they were capable? Because, you see gentlemen, these boys are now fertilizing daffodils. But if you listen real close, you can hear them whisper their legacy to you. Go on, lean in. *[the students lean in]* Listen, you hear it? *[Keaton whispering]* — Carpe — hear it? — Carpe, carpe diem, seize the day boys, make your lives extraordinary!"

Did the students in the pictures live up to all that they were capable of? We do not know. What we do learn is that Keating's new students start to learn the power of realizing their own potential. Often reciting the famous Latin mantra, "Carpe Diem" (or "Seize the Day") they slowly begin to believe that by taking advantage of each day they can live a life that is defined with significance and meaning. They each take risks and take advantage of pursuing opportune moments that come their way. One student ends up winning the heart of a girl way out

21

of his league while another discovers his burning passion to act in the theater. It is the combined effort of a group of youth who seek to fight conformity, think freely and live extraordinarily that makes Dead Poets Society a timeless, inspirational movie.

Carpe Diem

Watching the movie, I felt the horror of getting caught up in past mistakes or being enslaved to worry from focusing too much on the future. I was reminded of the importance of living solely for the present moment, for the "right now" moments of every day — the only moments within my control.

The adventurous, worry free life that God has for you and I is found in seizing every God-given moment of every God-given day.

Right now is the only reality you know and can live in. Think about it! The past has already happened and will never happen again. The future is always a day away; it is always out of our reach. All you have is right now.

And now.

And now.

And now.

And now I am wasting your time.

I have identified two factors that keep us from living fully in the moment. The first deals with the life behind you and the second is the life ahead.

Letting The Past Haunt Your Present

The beautiful thing about being a Christian is that you never have to let all the crap from the path behind you get flung onto the ground you walk on today. "Their sins and lawless acts I will remember no more.[16]" The Bible promises that, because of what Jesus has done on the cross, our sins are cast "as far as the east is from the west.[17]" You do not have to be a geography major to know that the east never meets the west. We will never be reacquainted with our sin of the past. In Christ, it is gone forever.

We must not let guilt and shame from the past come to rob us of the joy Christ offers us today. If you have confessed your sin to Him, as 1 John 1:9 promises, "He is faithful and just to forgive us our sins and cleanse us from all unrighteousness." In Christ, your past is cleansed and forgiven.

Learn from mistakes; do not dwell on them. Can you imagine a runner who runs his race constantly looking behind him? Of course not! He looks forward to where he is going — towards his destination. We are, as Paul says, "Forgetting what is behind and pressing on towards the goal for which God has called me heavenward in Christ Jesus[18]."

Not being preoccupied with the past, wanting to seize each moment, we need to start looking ahead. Sometimes the "ahead" part can be even more concerning than the stuff behind you. What do you do when the future is so unsettling?

Worry, Today's Number One Killer Of Teenage Joy

Having a goal for your life is important. I would never think to drive my car without having a destination in mind. Once I pick

---

[16]   Hebrews 10:17
[17]   Psalm 103:12
[18]   Phillipians 3:14

a place to go, I need to start planning the route. You should have goals for your life — a dream you think God wants you to accomplish while on earth. Guys, this is especially important if you want to be with a girl. She will be attracted to a compelling vision for your life but exponentially more so, *her dad* will demand you have a compelling vision for your life, especially if you want his consent to let her leave the house with you.

So what if you do not have a vision just yet. You are in your late teens and still are unsure how to answer the "what you are going to do after high school?" question.

That would make even the best of us start to perspire just a little.

Worry is a powerfully destructive tool that the enemy uses to rob us of our joy in the present. What do you worry about most?

What am I supposed to do with my life?
What if I don't get into the school I want?
What if I don't get a good job?
What if I don't get married?
What if I miss out on God's will for my life?

What if, what if, what if... I've seen these two words cause countless people to lose countless days or even entire years of their lives. I've seen fear intensified with students in their senior year of high school. With such a high demand for post secondary education, never before have grade twelve students felt such pressure to have their entire life mapped out before they walk across the platform at grad.

Everyone wants to know what you are going to do with your life, what school you're going to, what career you will have, etc. Chances are that you have already felt the aforementioned anxiety and the loneliness that comes with it. In trying to determine our own path we often incorrectly assume that everyone else has it already figured out (whatever "it" is). This can be a very scary, lonely place to be in — especially when clear answers are not coming.

I struggled a lot with worry while playing hockey. It was so consuming to me that I had "Proverbs 3:5–6" painted on the front of my mask to remind me each time I went on the ice that God was ultimately in control of my life and had my future taken care of. This verse, one of my favourites in the Bible reads, "Trust in the Lord with all of your heart and lean not on your own understanding. In all of your ways acknowledge him and he will make your path straight."

If God is your God, you need not worry about figuring out your future. Jesus promises this during the most famous sermon ever preached, the Sermon on the Mount.

> "So do not worry, saying, 'What shall we eat?' or 'What shall we drink?' or 'What shall we wear?' For the pagans run after all these things, and your heavenly Father knows that you need them. But seek first his kingdom and his righteousness, and all these things will be given to you as well[19]."

If you are a Christian, here is how you deal with worry — you don't. Worry is anxiousness, nervousness and fear about the future. God does not want these to cloud your vision of tomorrow. He wants you experiencing joy today. If God is who He says that He is, then He has got control of all the tomorrows and you need not worry.

That is why I feel it is so important to have a deep faith in God if you want to keep your sanity. If there is no God and if I am in control of my life, then I am in big trouble. No, if I am in control of my life, *then we are all* in big trouble. Atheists can worry

---

[19]   Matthew 6:33

because they have no reason *not* to be concerned about the future. This is why they worry about making sure they go to the right school right away to get the right job with the right salary and the right retirement package. It's all about control. They have no one else to trust but themselves and that takes a lot of faith. I couldn't do it myself. Not with the alternatives that Jesus promises.

> "Do not worry about anything but in everything by prayer and supplication present your requests to God[20]."

When Paul tells God's people not to worry about anything, I think he really means it. I did a word search on the word "everything" and it means just what I thought it meant — "all things."

God says that He himself will take care of you. The application of this truth is simple: you need not let worry steal your joy for one more day. With God as your leader, even when confusion is at its peak, there can always be a certainty in your *un*certainty. To be certain of God's character and His goodness to us means that we can look uncertainty in the eye and even flourish in it. Worry can be transformed into excited anticipation of what is to come.

If you are living your life fully devoted to God and His will for your life, He will take full responsibility for you. He's got you covered. He's in control. Now take a breath... and learn to relax a little.

Learning To Live A Little

There is a quality to life that is robbed by stress and worry steals our joy. Please, do not be in a hurry to grow-up and "get on with your life." Things are not always better when you get

---

[20]   Phillipians 4:6

older so enjoy your next days as a young adult. You do not need to be in a hurry to get a degree, get into a career or "settle down." You have the rest of your life to do those things and people that do rush in always wish they could go back.

You have time in the next formative years to live a little and find out who you are. I suggest you take some time to seriously find out what it is you like doing most and then see if it pays enough to make it into a career. School today is too expensive to just rush into. I suggest you work for a bit and then use the money to travel the world or get some buddies together and form a band. Go on tour for a couple of months living in a van. Take a year or two and work at an orphanage in Africa. Before having kids of your own, take care of those who will never see their parents again.

If you want to go the school route, keep options open: take a science, some english and you cannot go wrong with a psychology or philosophy course. If nothing else, they're really interesting.

Whatever you do, during your post high school years you will be gaining two things that will help you much more than any expensive piece of paper you get from four years in school: life experience and character. Any Tom, Dick or Harriet can get a degree these days if they have enough money. Because everyone is getting one, it does not guarantee you will always get the job you want. Life experience and character will give you an edge over the competition for any job.

Here's my example. Let's say you are one of ten applicants for a job you are very qualified for. Like you, the other nine have the required education credentials putting everyone on an even playing field. Because you took my advice and lived a little before you jumped into your career, your potential boss is thoroughly impressed by your commitment to volunteer work overseas and asks questions about that little addition to your resume that no one else has. Turns out he ends up hiring you because he thinks that the Spanish you learned during your time abroad may come in handy sometime. As you are cashing your first paycheque and driving home in your new Ferrari, you will be glad that you didn't rush into that career at 22 just because everyone else was.

Then you can pick me up and take me out for lunch, and that will be sufficient thanks for now.

This is how I counsel all of the worried grade twelve students I meet who think the world will pass them by and leave them homeless if they don't go to school right away.

What's the hurry really? In this season of life, you have the most free time and the least responsibility that you will ever have. Free time and no responsibility? It's fleeting and you only get it once so enjoy it now.

Go exploring; take road trips, boat trips, and plane trips. You can play in bands, act in plays, or volunteer anywhere. Learn an instrument or a few languages. Your youth is like a currency. You can spend it wherever and however you want. The problem is that you're running out of it a little more every day — so get moving.

The worst thing you can do is to throw these days away playing video games or watching TV and movies. That would be a tragedy. If playing video games is your idea of enjoying your youth, you need to grow-up, get a job and move out of your parent's house. In fact, don't even bother with the rest of this chapter. Just go get a job.

It is my presumption that every adult, including the writer of this book, wishes he or she could go back to the time of life that *you* are currently living in. I hear old people say, "Youth is wasted on the young." Perhaps one reason they say that is that they see the foolishness of young people today so caught up in and so stressed out by worry that they are throwing away the gift that is their youth.

Achieving The Goal And Losing The Journey

The problem is that we are all a product of a very goal-oriented culture. We are so focused on the future, that we lose the joy that comes in living in the moment. It's all about the destinations of life: graduating high school, graduating college, landing the job, getting married, having a family, retiring. They are all verbs, "doing words," by my grade three teacher's definition. Graduating isn't about getting a piece of paper; it is about going to class everyday, learning, being tested, and then doing that over and over again each day.

The destination is the goal but the journey is how you get there. The journey is the road to your destination and is where most of your life will be spent. It's full of twists and turns, ups and downs, and times of uncertainty and clarity. The journey can be sunny, rainy, snowy, and foggy and sometimes all at the same time. That's the part of life that you have to learn to enjoy because it is where you will do most of your living.

Along the way, it is okay to admit that things are unclear, that the path seems dark and yet still be completely fine with it. In such times, we could learn from the life of the Apostle Paul and how he stayed grounded when life seemed so up in the air for him.

Paul's Certainty In Uncertainty

The Bible gives us a backstage pass as to how the Apostle Paul, the great missionary, planned his future in regards to his destination and message. This story is from Acts 16:6–10 (if you have trouble reading big names in the Bible, the trick is to say them really fast):

"Paul and his companions traveled throughout the region of Phrygia and Galatia, having been kept by the Holy Spirit from preaching the word in the province of Asia. When they came to the border of Mysia, they tried to enter Bithynia, but the Spirit of Jesus would not allow them to. So they passed by Mysia and went down to Troas. During the night Paul had a vision of a man of Macedonia standing and begging him, 'Come over to Macedonia and help us.' After Paul had seen the vision, we got ready at once to leave for Macedonia, concluding that God had called us to preach the gospel to them."

This passage in Acts is a comedy sketch of biblical proportions. The more I think about this text, the more I realize that Paul, the one who is responsible for the spread of the early church and for writing most of the New Testament, wasn't always sure exactly what he was supposed to be doing.

I can picture Paul addressing his gang, "Okay fellas (wringing his hands with excitement), today we leave for a trip all the way to Asia... no, no, hold on a second. I think I'm hearing that it's now Mysia. Yes, we're going to Mysia. That's our spot.... What? Did you say Bithynia, Lord? Where's that? Okay, we're off to Bithynia! No? Yes? No? Oh... okay Mysia and then onto... Troas — did you say Troas? Never mind, let's call it a night boys. I'll sleep on it and get back to you in the morning."

It is safe to suggest that Paul had no idea where he was going a lot of the time. At first he was dead positive that he was to minister in Asia but then God put the brakes on that journey and it was over to Bithynia. Then he was directed otherwise by Jesus himself to go elsewhere. It wasn't until he was sound asleep that he ended up with the right marching directions.

Paul seemed fine with it though. Unlike us, my favourite apostle did not let worry take over when making decisions about his future. What's the secret, Paul? Paul lived his whole life in obedience to where he felt the Spirit of Jesus was telling him to go. Paul's heart was pointed straight at Jesus and that meant he was always in a good place regardless of where it took him. When Paul did not know where he was going, he knew who he was following. Because he knew Jesus would always take care of him, he did not freak out or take matters into his own hands.

You too can be certain of the love, goodness and care of the One you are following no matter how big your doubts are. So when you are asked that ever-annoying question about your future and you are not sure what to answer, I'm giving you permission to say,

"I'm not sure what's going to happen to me but I'm sure I'm following Jesus and He knows."

It's okay to confidently place your trust in the one who says, "I know the plans I have for you, plans to prosper you and not to harm you, to give you hope and a future[21]."

At Least Learn From This Jonathan
You know that moment of euphoria you often feel the moment that you meet someone with the same name as you? "Your name is Mark?...You will never believe this - My name is Mark too! Wow, that is absolutely amazing!" I have never been able to have such an experience with the man I am about to introduce you to. Though we share the same first name, Jonathan Edwards died over 250 years ago so he and I never had the chance to actually meet. Edwards was a fiery preacher who worked the preaching circuit out of New England in the United States. Edwards goes down as a hero in my books because he lived his life to the fullest as God's messenger for his entire life. Jonathan Edwards made resolutions in his early twenties

---

[21]   Jeremiah 29:11

to live intentionally for God's glory and God's glory alone. This made him one of the most influential preachers in history,.

Here are three of Edwards' famous resolutions that, if properly adapted to your own life, will guide you as you resolve to seize each day:

Resolution #5: "Resolved, never to lose one moment of time; but improve it the most profitable way I possibly can."

Resolution #6: "Resolved, to live with all my might, while I do live."

Resolution #17: "Resolved, that I will live so, as I shall wish I had done when I come to die[22]."

I am only slowly coming to grasp what it means to live fully in the moment — neither thinking about the past nor worrying about the future. I am inspired by men like Jonathan Edwards who have helped me with the slow learning process of living each day intentionally. Seizing the day does not just happen, it takes a strong commitment and determined follow through.

If you can live like this chapter proposes, you will never have to look back and wonder where the great days of your youth went. When you are all grown up with a career, screaming kids, car payments and a mortgage to pay, you won't wonder where your carefree, stress-free youthful days went. When you are old and grey, you will never have to sit back in your rocking chair and think your life was wasted.

You will have the satisfaction of knowing you accepted and lived each stage of life to its fullest potential. What a blessing it would be to make such a claim! It is certainly possible.

---

[22] Taken from Piper, John. *Don't Waste Your Life.* (Crossway Books, 2003)

So let's try this again: What are you going to do after high school?

Who knows? He knows! Yesterday is gone. Tomorrow will come. Today is all you can work with for now.

So go and seize it.

Carpe Diem.

This moment.

Right now.

That's what I wish for you. Now go play outside.

Getting Kicked Out Of Cool

And Being Grateful For It

"All that we call human history — money, poverty, ambition, war, prostitution, classes, empires, slavery — is the long terrible story of man trying to find something other than God which will make him happy."
C.S. Lewis, Mere Christianity

You have one life to live. You have one chance to walk this earth. There is a limited amount of time and that time gets shorter with every breath you take. What do you want to do with the rest of the breaths you take on earth?

Everybody wants his or her life to have meaning. God created you that way. He made us to search for meaning and wants us to journey with Him to discover it. The problem is that far too many of us never discover our God-given reason to be alive. Instead we settle for a mundane, watered down version of living that we've accepted for "just the way it is." 19th century American philosopher David Thoreau said, "the mass of men lead lives of quiet desperation."

This chapter is about your life: your one chance at living and the need to fight against the sin of "quiet desperation." This chapter is about the war going on between God, who wants to see you become all that He intended you to be, and the one who wants to steal, kill and destroy the life you were created to live.

This chapter is about breaking out from the masses in despair and really living.

What Do You Want To Be When You Grow Up?

I remember being asked that all the time. As kids, we all had big dreams for our lives. What did you dream about doing "when you grew up?" I'm talking about after those really early years when all you wanted to be was Sponge Bob or the colour orange. What did you see yourself doing? Astronaut, Doctor, Rock Star, Professional Athlete, Explorer, Dancer, Video Game Tester, Movie Star, Artist, Teacher, Plumber; all were popular choices amongst kids. We make it through high school and graduate trying to hold on to our childhood dreams, wondering if they are actually attainable. Walking across the stage on grad night, we are ready to do great things with our lives; we are optimistic about making it all happen.

Some people follow through on their dreams, and others do not. Why do some people see their dreams realized while others merely settle for second or third best? Something happens as you go through life that makes you want to give up on following the exciting and meaningful dreams you have now in order to follow the status quo of doing what everyone else is doing.

My nurse friends have confirmed for me that there exists a medical condition called "Failure To Thrive" which is diagnosed in infants who are not able to gain weight or experience physical growth over a period of time. Failure To Thrive or FTT is an interesting title, one that could be given to many adults. These are the people who settle for a life of simply earning a paycheque; they never step out and do what they were truly made to do. Look around you. Are there any adults in your life right now that you would diagnose with FTT? Don't start pointing but just start asking, "What do you think got them there?" What will stop you from catching this highly contagious pandemic sweeping through the suburban populace?

Everyone wants to thrive! Everyone wants to have meaning. They want to do what they love and find purpose in it. So how do people get like this? How do they go from being excited graduates full of dreams to the lifeless masses we see living in quiet desperation all around us?

Maybe it's time for a made-up story to help understand why competent, rational people end up wasting their one chance at life.

The Story Of Jamie and Jenny

Jamie was a bright honour roll student who graduated from high school really excited about all this new freedom he was getting. Freed from the shackles of institutionalized education, Jamie could do anything with his life and was excited to start pursuing things he was passionate about. Music was Jamie's main passion; he loved listening to it, playing it and teaching others how to play some of the many instruments he knew. In grade 10, Jamie was told by his teacher that many kids in poor communities could not afford music lessons because of the high cost of teachers. Jamie's dream since that conversation was to set up a music school in a poor community so kids could get a good musical education and find hope in overcoming poverty's cycle through music. Jamie understood this career path wasn't going to make him much money but it was going to make the world better and that's what mattered to our budding hero.

The summer after grad, Jamie's dad got him a job cutting grass for the city and, for the first time in his life, he was starting to accumulate money. Everyday he showed up to work in his ten year old car, his work buddies made fun of him. Because nobody likes being made fun of, he committed to saving up enough for a down payment on a new truck. After making a small down payment, Jamie took out a 5 year loan to pay off the rest. His friends liked the truck and a few high-fives later, Jamie was officially welcomed into the land of "Cool."

The problem with Jamie's entrance into the world of Cool is that it is an all-demanding world. You can't just be Cool in one place; you have to be Cool in all parts of life. Sure, Jamie's truck may have earned him some street credit with his coworkers, but they soon found something new to tease him about — his old cell phone.

Jamie's phone was *over two years old*. His friends had the latest and greatest phones; the kind you see on the commercials. They played Music, had Internet, TV, and GPS. Not wanting to fall behind, Jamie went to the mall and locked himself into a three-year contract with the phone company so he too could have a nice new phone. At the mall, Jamie picked up a new shirt and shoes because his old ones were no longer acceptable weekend attire in the world of Cool. He paid for it on his credit card knowing that he would be able to wear the clothes today with the money he would make tomorrow.

Years later, Jamie was still at his city job locked into payment plans for his truck, cell phone and credit card. He still had the dream of one day opening up a music school for poor students but that was still a few years away of course. Though working for the city was not his favourite line of work, it would not be long until he finally got started on the music school.

Jamie found himself a nice girlfriend named Jenny who was also from the world of Cool and, a couple years later, they got married. They committed to having their wedding in the land of Cool even though Cool weddings cost much more than weddings anywhere else. The tough part about a Cool wedding is that everything had to be more lavish and Cool than the previous wedding. There was always a great deal of pressure on the bride to outdo the last Cool bride — to have nicer dresses, a classier venue, fancier decorations, more tender meat, etc. As a result, the cost of Cool Weddings only continued to go up and up, and the pressure to impress Cool friends and Cool family created a lot of tension for Jamie and Jenny — especially when it came to paying for it all.

Not wanting to be kicked out of Cool for having a shameful wedding, Jamie and Jenny pulled off the finest wedding in Cool history. Thankfully, Jamie got a promotion at the city and was able to use his wage increase to help ease some of the financial burden as long as he worked longer hours at the office. He still didn't like his job, but it would help pay the bills and keep his Cool new wife happy for a while.

With the promotion came a change in friends for Jamie. No longer did he work with grass cutting teenagers, but found himself fraternizing with a group of middle class adults whose favourite topics included "The State Of The Market" and "What colour to paint the new garage door." Jamie realized the he had discovered a new class in the world of Cool: The Homeowners. Being a non-homeowner, Jamie found himself slowly being filtered out of Cool. Unless Jamie and Jenny moved quickly, other Cool people would replace them.

Jamie and Jenny found a realtor and bought a house that looked like every other house in their neighbourhood. Like the truck, the phone, the wedding and pretty much everything else they had bought, Jamie and Jenny learned that in the world of Cool, you could easily buy stuff now and pay for it later. Jamie agreed to work with the city a littler longer to cover the mortgage. It would be paid off in 40 years, leaving enough time after to start the music business for poor kids.

The neighbours in the Cool area were very nice but found new things to talk about. They loved their shiny new things: cars, BBQs, TVs. Jamie wanted badly to'talk about his new shiny things too so he took out another loan and bought two nice shiny cars. Soon enough they were active participants in the Cool shiny car talk.

Jamie had to work more to pay for the cars and no longer had time to play music. Now he only played the radio on the way to and from work. Jamie and Jenny made it a tradition to watch TV shows every night as a way to relax after their long days of work. During their favourite shows, Jamie and Jenny saw all sorts of Cool ads with Cool people doing Cool things. Like the average couple in Cool, they would see over 3,000 of these advertisements per day. The ads promised that if Jamie and Jenny bought Cool things, they would be happy and Cool for their whole lives.

Jamie wanted a Cool new TV; Jenny wanted a Cool dress; Jamie wanted a Cool phone; Jenny wanted a Cool Ikea kitchen. To afford these things, they each decided to work just a little harder and just a little longer.

Coming home from work after even longer hours, they were even more tired and had to watch even more TV that caused them to watch even more Cool ads with more Cool things could make them happy. They decided that if they worked harder and longer, they could have more of these Cool things they saw in the Cool ads.

Eventually Jamie and Jenny had some kids. They wanted to have Cool kids with Cool clothes and Cool strollers. Of course all these Cool things took more money and more work to buy, but that was the price everyone was paying to be a part of Cool in those days. It was okay because they always found new credit cards to help buy Cool things.

Jamie and Jenny were soon drowning in house payments, car payments, credit card payments, and the interest that went along with each of them. Trying to keep up with it all left the couple exhausted, and each wondered how living in Cool had become so expensive and tiring.

Jamie didn't even have the energy to talk about opening a school anymore.

Their kids grew up and were told they could dream big dreams and do whatever they wanted with their life. Jamie was filled with great hope when his son Jake said that he wanted to open up a music school for poor kids to get lessons when he grew up.

But until then, Jake would just take the job that his dad got him cutting grass for the city...

The Land Of Cool Is A Lie

What if, at some point, Jamie and Jenny had realized that their entire lives were part of a big lie? In February of 2001, the US public broadcasting channel, PBS, aired a documentary called *Merchants Of Cool*[23], which gave the public a backstage pass into how big corporations manipulate what is "cool" to get us to buy whatever it is they are selling. Consumers love cool. Cool is what drives the economy! The problem with cool is that it started inside a market research office. A bunch of people in business suits got together and brainstormed ways to shape our culture. *Merchants Of Cool* reports that the primary culture makers in Western society are five major corporations who are all vying for the hundreds of billions of dollars in consumer spending each year (the vast majority coming from teenagers). If these businesses can convince the public, through mainstream

---

[23] For more information on Merchants of Cool check out the website *(http://www.pbs.org/wgbh/pages/frontline/shows/cool/view/)*

media, celebrity endorsements and the three thousand subtle advertisements that we will process today that their product is "cool," then we, the public, will respond by throwing our billions of dollars directly at them. This is not ethical in my mind, but it is good business. If we are all stupid enough to continually hand them our money, I can't really blame them for picking it up and putting it in the bank.

Media critic Mark Crispin-Miller summarizes the market of Cool,

> "You know, advertising has always sold anxiety and it certainly sells anxiety to the young. It's always telling them that they are not thin enough, they're not pretty enough, they don't have the right friends, or they have no friends... they're losers unless they're cool. But I don't think anybody, deep down, really feels cool enough, ever."

All Jamie and Jenny wanted was to not be losers, and to keep their friends by keeping up with what everyone else was doing. In reality, they were just puppets who had surrendered their unique hopes, dreams and credit cards. It did not happen overnight either. For this fictitious couple, one decision to be cool led to another and, all of a sudden, their lives got very predictable and boring. Wake up, go to work, watch TV, and go to bed. Next day: wake up, go to work, watch TV, and go to bed. Next day: wake up...

You get the idea. At some point, if you're Jamie, you wake up wondering, "What has happened to my life? Where did my dreams go? Why did I buy all this crap? Who told me that I needed it all?"
Jesus said, "I have come that you may have life and have it to the full[24]." Fullness of life, excitement, and adventure; that is

---

[24]   John 10:10

Jesus' offer. The problem is that we don't all choose that kind of life.

E.E. Cummings said, "To be yourself in a world that is trying to make you like everyone else is to fight the hardest battle anyone can fight."

Mark my words, without a fight your life *will* become boring, predictable and just like everyone else. I think too many people in our culture are content just hanging out in the land of Cool. It kills them, but they're okay with that because it's what we're told is normal and they just want to blend in.

I like the Message translation of this verse from 1 Peter, "Your life is a journey you must travel with a deep consciousness of God. It cost God plenty to get you out of that dead-end, empty-headed life you grew up in. He paid with Christ's sacred blood[25]." Our culture supports dead-ended, empty-headed living. Thinking about your life right now? It sounds so tragic to think that you could turn out like Jamie and Jenny. If you do not make a conscious effort to fight it, you will write the exact same story as they.

You're Unique, Just Like Everybody Else

I once heard Donald Miller, author of the bestselling book Blue Like Jazz, speak about the necessity of a character in a story having a compelling objective to accomplish for it to be a good story. For instance, the story of a man saving a child's life makes for a good story. A man saving $500 in the bank will gain interest but not the kind that a successful author is looking for. A story about a guy buying a car is not as engaging for an audience as a story about a guy driving a car to stop a bomb from going off in a crowded area. If nobody is crying and clapping at the end of your life story, you have a lame story.

---

[25]   1 Peter 1:18 *The Message*

"Oh wow... so he finally managed to pay off his mortgage, retired and played golf (wipe away a tear)... that's... that's just a beautiful story."

It has happened to most of us at some point when we see a great preview for a movie — the anticipation nearly kills us and when we watch it in the theatre, we find out it is actually a real stinker. Nobody ever leaves a movie theater at the end of a bad movie and concludes, "All movies are meaningless!" No, instead we walk out and conclude, "That movie was meaningless."

If your life seems like it lacks excitement, adventure or anything worth remembering, chances are that it may not be the best conclusion for you to say "All life is meaningless!" Instead the more fitting description would be that "Your life is meaningless."

Of course, you never wanted your life to be void of meaning; we already talked about how there is a deep need in every human to live a life of purpose and significance during our time on earth. God intended great things of eternal impact; the enemy wants to destroy that dream of God's.

We lose our original God given dream and settle for a meaningless life when we try to live in Cool. Jesus says that the road to Hell is wide and it's really easy to find — just do what everyone else is doing. The way to finding the narrow road, the path to life and to discovering that you were made for something different, is to know that God did not make you to be like everyone else. He has made you incredibly unique. Since the very beginning of your life when you were still cooking in your mother's womb, God had a plan for you — the one and only you in the history of the world. God crafted you with distinct gifts, abilities and then lined up experiences that make you one of a kind. We are God's workmanship, his masterpiece[26].

---

[26]   Ephesians 2:10

The most boring thing about you is your name and where you were born. Your life has a story that God wants you to tell the world. That's not just some "make you feel good" postmodern psychobabble; that is the truth.

It is important to make sure you fight the temptation when hearing these kinds of truths so that you avoid self-centeredness and pride. God crafted you and gifted you with unique abilities to be used for His glory and His fame--not your own. You were made to reflect your Creator. Mirrors never get any of the credit for the beauty they show. It is always directed back to the original image.

How serious does God take it that we use our God-given uniqueness to its fullest potential? Let's look at what He said to a bunch of people who did not achieve such a feat.

A Lesson From The Laodiceans

The more I learn about the book of Revelation, the more I think it is one of the greatest, yet all too often misunderstood, gems of the New Testament. Revelation 3:17–22 is a letter written to the Church in a city called Laodicea. In it we see Jesus' sharp rebuke to a church that was so rich and in love with its culture that it had become useless to Him and His purposes for them. Jesus said to His people,

"Here I am, I stand at the door and knock[27]." Jesus was not invited to a meeting called in His name. Picture him standing outside knocking on the door waiting for someone to let Him in.

If you are old enough to remember the cartoon, *The Flintstones* then you will recall the very end of the closing song when Fred attempts to leave the cat outside for the night only to have the

---

[27]   Revelation 3:20

cat jump back into the house where it manages to close and lock the door. In effect, Fred has been left outside for the night instead of the cat. The song ends with Fred pounding on the door of his own house yelling, "Wilma!"

Jesus also calls to the Laodiceans from outside the door, "Hey guys, I built this place, remember? My picture is over there on the wall... Can I come in?"

We treat Jesus this way when we get so obsessed with blending in with our culture and forget about Jesus and his counter-cultural purposes for our lives and our churches. We think we are doing just fine but Jesus sees it a different way.

> "You say 'I am rich; I have acquired wealth and do not need a thing.' But you do not realize that you are wretched, pitiful, poor, blind and naked[28]."

These Christians that Jesus was talking to were very confused. Because of their great wealth, they believed themselves in want of nothing. Jesus couldn't disagree more, choosing adjectives such as "wretched, poor, blind and naked" to describe them. This is what happens when Christians try to live in Cool; they get made fun of by Jesus.

> "I know your deeds, that you are neither cold nor hot. I wish you were one or the other! So, because you are lukewarm — neither hot nor cold — I am about to spit you out of my mouth[29]."

When sitting through sermons preached on Jesus words to the Laodiceans, these words always confused me. I was taught that the reason why Jesus is angry here is because of those no-good fence-sitters; the Laodiceans were not hot and passionate for Jesus nor were they cold for the things of Christ.

---

[28] Revelation 3:17
[29] Revelation 3:15-16

The big idea was always, "Are you all for Jesus or all against him? You can choose one but not both, and whatever you do, do not be lukewarm."

I didn't get why Jesus would want people to be so devilishly cold. Doesn't He desire "that none should perish?" It did not make sense to me why Jesus would want people playing for the wrong team.

When you study the ancient city of Laodicea, the real meaning of this passage becomes much more interesting and even more convicting. Laodicea was a very affluent city much like our culture today. Despite the wealth, the original founders mistakenly built the city at a vast distance from any major body of water. This caused a big problem for people who lived there as water is a necessity for human survival. Because they had money, Laodiceans built expensive aqueducts to transport water in. Outside Laodicea were the hot springs of Hieropolis, whose warm water was famous for its healing purposes in those days. Think of the relaxation of relaxing in a hot tub and then think of Hieropolis. Also, the aqueducts from the Springs of Colossae supplied Laodicea with cold spring water — good for a refreshing drink. The problem with transporting your water via the aqueduct system in those days was the exposure to the elements during the water's lengthy travel. By the time the hot water arrived in Laodicea it had time to cool and was no longer hot. It was the same with the cold water of Colossae — it warmed up in the sun. The hot water cooled and the cold water warmed up. Both aqueducts brought in a fresh supply of lukewarm water.

The hot water was no longer good for healing and the cold water was too warm to be refreshing. They were both useless. Nobody likes a tall glass of warm water on a hot day. You spit that stuff out!

So does Jesus.

I sense that Jesus is saying to the Laodicean church and to all of us, "You have compromised with your culture. You are useless — your purpose can not be accomplished like this. You were supposed to be different — unique — in order to show the world what I look like. Instead, you do not look like me; you look like everyone else. So I'm going to spit you out."

Those are tough words. Jesus is serious in His desire that we live lives of purpose and effectiveness so that we can do what He created us to do.

Are you hot, cold, or lukewarm? What do you think Jesus would say if He wrote a letter to your church?

What do you think Jesus would say if He wrote a letter to you about your life?

How To Rip Up Your Invitation To Cool

John the Baptist was a different kind of guy. He called the people to prepare for the coming of Jesus by telling them to repent from following the sinful ways of the world. John lived in the hot and dry Judean desert. His diet consisted of grasshoppers smothered in fresh honey (Yum!). John was not into the latest fashions of his era choosing instead to don homemade camel hair that would make even Ghandi look metro. John was okay being different; he was a revolutionary. He knew the dress code and understood the cultural rules but he refused to play by them. John was a leader; he would have known better than to think that buying the new iPod was going to make him happy. John lived simply, avoiding the snare of material things, in order to do what God wanted him to do with his life.

There are other Bible heroes that God called to be different; in fact, He did it a lot. Jacob, Rahab, Jonah, Isaiah, Ezekiel, Jeremiah, Esther, Hosea, Daniel, Paul are just a few of the many great men and women that God asked to do some radical, often unpopular, things. It was worth the cost for the trajectory of their lives and the course of world history was forever changed. The problem is that they all got kicked out of Cool for it. I suppose they did not really care about that though.

My prayer is that God would raise up a generation who will deny the invitation to live in the land of Cool. They will still love Cool people but will refuse to get sucked into their destructive, self-centered habits.

God is calling rebels in our midst today. It used to be that rebels were the type who wore leather jackets, rode motorcycles, smoked Marlboro cigarettes and drank cheap domestic beer. Today's rebels are the people who look at their world critically and observe the patterns of a destructive consumeristic lifestyle and its spending habits. They see the empty promises of Cool for the lies that they are. Today's rebels choose to live counter culturally. They see the masses simply going along with the current, and choose instead to swim upstream no matter how tiring it may get.

Dare To Be Different

If you're up for the challenge, here are eight ways I am proposing that you can be a rebel in the 21st century. Of course, your ideas and application may look completely different than mine. These are just some suggestions I thought you should consider:

1. Live On Less.

If you figure out just how destructive our consumer culture really is, you will discover just how little you need. You know that new cell phone you think you need which does the same stuff as your old cell phone but has a better camera and is a different color? You don't need it. So before you go buy something, ask yourself the tough questions: Do I really need this? What is this purchase promising to deliver to me? Will it deliver what I am really looking for?

49

I love what St. Francis of Assisi says, "I own nothing that I might enjoy everything." When you live simply, you don't get burdened with debts, loans and payments. You just buy what you can afford and as little as you need.

Here is an equation worth remembering: $5 earned - $7 spent= Unhappy Life.

Picture every thing you buy coming with a string that ties itself to you. The more stuff you have, the more strings get attached to you. With more strings come more restrictions and less mobility. We like to think that we own all our stuff but actually our stuff starts to own us after awhile. We forget that everything actually belongs to God who gives stuff to us in order that we might take care of it and even share our stuff with others. That is why those who have the least possessions are the most generous people. They have not let their things own them and can freely share. A.W. Tozer calls this, "the blessedness of possessing nothing[30]." There is a great blessing in owning few things. Learn to live on as little as possible and very little will own you.

I mention this because the time is coming, or maybe it has already come, when a credit card offer will come in the mail. An accountant I know says that rather than calling these "credit cards," we should call them, "debt cards." Some guys in suits at a bank got together and decided to lend you some money that you don't have just yet. This card offer will be your introduction to the "Buy now, pay later" mentality which brings with it many, many strings that a young person may not have the maturity or discipline to endure. I'm not against credit cards, but make sure you have the money to back up your spending.

And always make your monthly payment. It will help you in the long run. If you cannot pay off your expenses, cut up the card, pay it off and stop buying things you cannot pay for.
Resist the temptation to buy on credit. Live simply.

---

[30] Tozer, A.W. *The Pursuit Of God* (Christian Publications, 1993)

2. Be Willing To Fail.

The fear of failure keeps people living their boring lives. Too many in our culture are absolutely paralyzed by a fear of failure and so they never try to live out their God-given dreams. They are scared to fail, look bad or end up broke and living on the streets. Instead of risking failure, they settle in the Land of Cool and know nothing but the boredom of a life full of the routine, the safe and the familiar.

I grew up reading this quote from Theodore Roosevelt that my dad had posted on his wall, and I would encourage you to post it somewhere to remind you that it's okay to risk big, fail big and be mocked. At least you are among the few who try and, according to Roosevelt, for that you are worthy of honour.

> "It is not the critic who counts; nor the man who points out how the strong man stumbles, or where the doer of deeds could have done them better. The credit belongs to the man who is actually in the arena, whose face is marred by dust and sweat and blood, who strives valiantly; who errs and comes short again and again; because there is not effort without error and shortcomings… who at the best knows in the end the triumph of high achievement and who at the worst, if he fails, at least he fails while daring greatly. So that his place shall never be with those cold and timid souls who know neither victory nor defeat[31]."

Robert Guizeta, CEO of Coca Cola from 1980–1997, has a remarkable story of overcoming failure in life. He said, "Remember if you take risks, you may still fail, but if you do not take risks you will surely fail. The greatest risk of all is to do nothing[32]." Some people are so worried about looking bad that they will not try anything that involves any element of

---

[31] Roosevelt, Theodore. From a speech in Paris on April 23, 1910 called "Citizenship in a Republic"

[32] See article at *http://www.livinglifefully.com/risk.htm*

risk. Sure, with risk comes the potential to fail and with failure comes the potential to look bad. Failure can be a really good thing, however. My greatest lessons in life have been when I have taken great risks, tried the impossible, and fallen flat on my face.

It is inevitable that you will fail at many things throughout your life. It is coming — learn to handle it well. Realize that when you run hard, you will sometimes fall down. Only good can come from getting up, brushing off the dirt, cleaning up the blood and starting to run again. Be thankful that you just learned another lesson in how to run properly.

3. Have Courage.
Have the guts to know the truth in your heart — you will not be defined by your possessions or by anything other than God. You are a child of God — that is what He calls you and that is who you are. You are not the car you drive, the house you live in, the amount of money in your bank account, or the clothes you wear. Those things do not make a person more or less important. They do not add or lessen the value found in human life.

Have the courage to live the truth and to see others in the same light.

4. Do Christmas Different.
We have distorted Christmas into a funny and horrible monster. Shopping. The stress. Malls. Credit Card debt. Greed. Seriously, how can we call it "giving a gift" when you make a list of things you want and tell someone to give those things to you? Is that what Christmas is? Read the story. You don't see anywhere in the gospel account where the wisemen come up to baby Jesus and then present *each other* with gifts. They do bring gifts, yes, but they are for *Jesus*, the King, not each other! They worship Him. Be different and make Christmas about the birth of Jesus and not about getting stuff.

5. Have Some Perspective.

When building any sort of structure today, everything has to be treated, as per the city code, with strict fire retardant chemicals that prevent the structure from bursting into flames in the unfortunate occurrence of a fire. Though fire retardant may hold off the flames for a while, nothing is completely fire proof in the end. The Bible promises that the ultimate destiny of all our stuff on earth is fuel for fire. According to 2 Peter 3:7, everything is going to be burned up one day. "By the same word the present heavens and earth are reserved for fire, being kept for the Day of Judgment and destruction of ungodly men."

Your new iPod you worked so hard to get will one day be used as kindling. That closet of clothes you love so much, the video games, DVD collections, cars, houses… everything will go up in flames.

That should give you a little bit of heaven's perspective. Charles Spurgeon got really practical and encouraged his congregation to put little notes on all their stuff that said, "To be burned one day." Want to get really practical? I dare you to take a few sticky notes with the same words written on them and start putting them on all your precious possessions.

6. Prepare For Eternity.

Think of the chronological span of eternity as a line that goes on forever. In light of eternity, our time on earth is incredibly short. To think that our brief moments here will determine where and how we spend eternity puts a lot of importance on how we live today.

During my short, three week trip to the Gambia in Africa, I knew that my time there was limited. The trip was so short it would have been foolish of me to act like the Gambia was a long-term home. I didn't built a house, buy a car, or sign a long-term cell phone contracts while I was there. I was constantly aware of the brevity of my stay and that affected the way I lived each day. My conversations were intentional; I tried to help whoever, however, I could. Each day was a new chance to grow in my love for God and to share His love with all I met. I could put up with not having my own bed with my own sheets and pillow; I didn't need my Starbucks coffee and I could put up with food that I did not like at all. I did this because I knew it was temporary and I would be back home one day.

It's the same with Christians and the hope of heaven. We are to live like this world is passing away and that heaven is our real home. It's the people that live like this that are the most fun and exciting people to be around. They live the most rewarding lives because they don't care about rewards here. When people live for heaven, nothing on this earth can own them and nothing can stop them from their mission of knowing God and making Him known. They know that to be human on earth is not about your collection of stuff, your entertainment, or your anything really. It is to be about Him and others. May we all live our lives with eternity at the forefront of our minds. How different would our churches look if the people of God actually lived like this?

7. Be Grateful.
At what point will you have enough? "Enough" is a great word that we should all learn. One day you need to declare that what you have is good enough to live on and that adding anything else is not going to make you happy. Turn on the tap and thank God that you are among the most fortunate people in the world who can get clean drinking water from a tap. Drive your old car and be thankful that you are wealthy enough to afford it. Be grateful you have shelter over your head. Be grateful for the clothes in your closet. Be grateful for the food in your stomach and the food in the fridge. If you have meat in your sandwich tomorrow, say a prayer of thanks for the standard of living that you enjoy. You have enough. Are you grateful for it?

8. Give Away More.
Every time you give away money or make financial sacrifices, you chip away at that big ugly monster of consumerism that has its grip on so many North Americans today. Jesus says, "Where your treasure is, there your heart will be also." Your money will follow your heart. Give to your church and watch your passion grow for the church. Give to an organization that fights poverty or disease and watch your heart begin to break for the things that break God's heart. You can be free from the tyranny of selfish consumeristic hoarding by giving away your time, talent and treasure. When you give, your attention is diverted away from yourself towards a person, a cause, or a vision much bigger than just yourself. That's how you do it. Give generously and watch your heart begin to change.

What Road Will You Choose?
We started this chapter by asking, "What will you do with the one chance you have been given to live your life?" There are two roads — one is wide and easy to find. It is a road with a lot of traffic and is soft underfoot. There you will find Jamie, Jenny and all their Cool friends who value conformity, consumption, safety and image.

The second road is narrow; there are not a lot of people walking it because it is tough to find and hard to walk. Those on this road value contentment, uniqueness, simplicity, clarity and sacrifice.

It is the road that leads out of the make-believe land of Cool and into true life. How will you live the rest of your one chance at life? The choice is yours.

Bad Preaching Scared The Hell Out Of The Church

How The World Got So Messed Up

"Some have staggered over the doctrine of eternal punishment, because they could not see how that could be consistent with God's goodness. I have only one question to ask concerning that or any other doctrine - Does God reveal it in the Scriptures? If so, then, I believe it, and leave to him the vindication of his own consistency."
- Charles Haddon Spurgeon

You have probably already noticed that the world is messed up. Something has gone horribly wrong.

Each day, the newspapers and their respective reporters give us brand new stories to throw on the pile of this "messed-upness." These stories include the following themes (just to name a few): murder, poverty, injustice, rape, greed, crime, violence, bullying and brokenness. No matter what your geographical, cultural or religious background, you have probably come to the conclusion that things are not as they might be on planet Earth. As you get older, you will be exposed to and witness horrific acts of evil done by people to people, and by people to themselves.

This chapter will help you make sense of why human beings behave as poorly as they do. It could get depressing but it will help you make sense of how things came to be the way they are and who is to blame for humanity's condition.

Back To The Beginning

The first book of the Bible is Genesis, which means "Beginnings." Genesis is the account of how God got things started. After He created the world, God created the first man and woman (Adam and Eve) and placed them in a beautiful garden (Eden). He tells them they are free to eat from all of the trees in the garden except for one tree — the tree of the knowledge of good and evil and He promises that disobedience to His one rule will come with a severe consequence.

"If you eat of this tree, you will surely die.[33]"

God is telling Adam and Eve, "I am the source of all life, joy, love, peace and freedom. Turn to me and your life will be full of those things. If you turn away from me, you will experience the opposite: death, pain, sorrow, slavery, anxiety, and oppression. It's your call."

Here are a few questions that might help you identify with Adam and Eve. When you were a kid, did your mom ever leave a plate of cookies on the counter and give you strict orders not to eat them? What was it that made you want to eat those cookies so very badly? Was it the thought of the cookie taste touching your mouth? Was it because you were told not to? Perhaps it was a combination of the two.

The Garden of Eden was huge; Adam and Eve could have gone anywhere to avoid the temptation to break God's one law. The forbidden fruit in the story, however, represented many

---

[33]   Genesis 2:17

things: immediate gratification to a real hunger, a chance to make decisions independently of God and the pride of being as knowledgeable as God. It was more than a piece of forbidden fruit. It looked like the sweet taste of freedom. Here's what happened:

"When Eve saw that the fruit was pleasing to the eye and good for eating, she took of it and ate[34]."

It was rebellion against God and that rebellion was the introduction of sin to the world. Sin is telling God that we know better than He does. Sin is feeling like God is holding out on you and then doing something about it yourself. This is exactly what Eve did when she took and ate the forbidden fruit.

A Broken Law And A Broken Relationship

I think a major human milestone to the growing up process is getting your first speeding ticket. I got mine very shortly after I got my driver's license. As a brand new driver, I did not have my parents' full trust. As a result, I was told by my mom that I could drive her car as long as I stuck to an agreed upon route that led directly to my friend's house and back. Being a brand new driver, I soon grew discontent with the agreed upon route. I had spent most of my driver's training with my parents riding shotgun, which meant that my speed had been heavily monitored for the entirety of my short driving career. Sticking to my mom's route felt restrictive and slightly boring, so I decided to take a small detour and prolong the novelty of the driving experience. A straight section of road just off the predetermined course was my perfect opportunity to experiment with the 1.6 L 102 Horsepower engine in Mom's 1991 Toyota Corolla. My freedom was exhilarating! But as I have learned many times since then, there are often consequences for my wayward actions.

---

[34]   Genesis 3:6

So what were the chances that during my first taste of vehicular freedom there would be a police car passing me on the other side of the road? On that night, apparently my odds were pretty good. The police car's lights went on, the officer turned the car around and I nearly threw up all over my mom's finely upholstered Corolla seats. In my youthful anxiety, I managed to utter an apology and hoped that the man in blue would extend me a gracious acquittal. However, his fount of grace was dry that day and I was issued my very first of many speeding tickets.

My little racing experience in my mom's Corolla broke a couple of agreements that I had entered into on that particular day. First, I broke the provincial laws of British Columbia. I chose not to obey a set of rules established by a group of educated folks, who determined an appropriate and rational speed limit for the purpose of keeping me safe on that particular section of road. Therefore, when I decided to drive above the posted speed limit, I broke the law of our land and paid for it in the form of a $173 ticket. (For any of you who are wondering about the fall out with my parents after the speeding ticket incident, here is a short synopsis. I told my parents about the incident and we're totally cool now).

Second, I also broke the verbal contract that I had with my mom, which could have had a detrimental impact on my relationship with her. By driving outside of the agreed upon route and speeding along merrily, I broke her trust. I thought I knew what was better for me and I got busted.

I think my story is similar to the situation that Adam and Eve found themselves in when they disobeyed God — both a law and a relationship were broken. When we sin against God, not only are we breaking the rules He has made for our benefit, but we are also breaking the relationship with the One who loves us enough to make the rules in the first place! God's laws reflect

God's character, and by breaking God's laws we violate our relationship with Him. Sin will always cut us off from Him.

Eve knew that. She knew what was at stake because she was warned beforehand about the consequences of eating the forbidden fruit. She knew she would be breaking her relationship with God. She thought that she knew more than God and had a better way to live. Are any of us any different in our sin?

The Sin Of Silent Adam

Eve was not the only person involved with the first sin. Adam, Eve's husband, was watching as she turned her back on the Creator. While Eve's was a sin of commission (she ate the fruit), Adam's was a sin of omission (he just sat there and watched it happen). He did not eat the forbidden fruit, do drugs, say naughty swears or get drunk. Adam's sin was that of being passive, lazy and unwilling to fight or to speak up. This is sin as well. Silent Adam's sin can be summed up with these words:

"She gave some to her husband, *who was with her*[35]."

Adam did nothing! He just stood there and watched it all happen and then even took a bite himself. When men watch evil happen in their world and do nothing about it, they prove that they are no different than their first father, Adam. These sons of Adam are quick to quit, abandon, and avoid responsibility. They say nothing, do nothing, involve themselves in nothing and accomplish nothing. "One of the greatest problems in the world," says Pastor Mark Driscoll, "is men who are like Adam. You do nothing at all. You are silent, passive cowards."

Adam and Eve disobeyed God in different ways but they each share the blame for our separation from Him in the present and for eternity. They ate the cookies. They knew what they were

---

[35]   Genesis 3:6

doing and they did it anyway. Blatantly ignoring what God says makes Him upset to the point of anger.

The Punishment For Disobeying Your Creator

God gave one order, "don't eat this fruit," and they did it anyway. At this point, what was God to do knowing that His creation had just totally ignored Him? He warned Adam and Eve that sin would have mortal consequences and they didn't seem to care. Should God simply throw up his hands, laugh awkwardly and say, "Ha ha... Just kidding guys! When I said you would die for your disobedience, what I *really* meant is that nothing would happen! You called my bluff; good for you."

God never bluffs. He means what He says — "The wages of sin is death[36]." Here are the consequences that Adam and Eve experienced because of their poor decisions.

> "Cursed is the ground because of you; through painful toil you will eat of it all the days of your life. It will produce thorns and thistles for you, and you will eat the plants of the field. By the sweat of your brow you will eat your food until you return to the ground, since from it you were taken; for dust you are and to dust you will return[37]."

This is ugly stuff. God pronounces a curse on the created world because of the first man and woman's disobedience. In short, here are the results: having a baby will cause a lot of pain and gender roles will be confused. The ground, necessary for making food, is also cursed. Work will not be fun; rather it will be quite sweaty and stinky. From the earth will come tornados and hurricanes that destroy cities, earthquakes that kill tens of thousands and tsunamis that kill hundreds of thousands.

---

[36]   Romans 6:24
[37]   Genesis 3:17-19

Humanity will be born with a fatal disease that will increase the human mortality rate to a consistent 100%.

The original sin of Adam and Eve has caused more problems than we can count, and the ripple effect continues into the present day. Moreover, we continue to add to the world's sin-problems with our own sin.

Our history books are plagued with stories of violence, war, abuse, disease, poverty, rape, genocide and many more problems that result from the sinful nature of man. Unless we understand the full extent of the fall of Adam and Eve, we will never understand why these sorts of things happen in our educated, postmodern civilization. Sin continues to affect each generation and it will continue to reach us here in the 21st century — on the news, in our communities and in our hearts.

No matter where I have been in the world, I have observed that sin has permeated everything. Corrupt governments get rich while their population starves to death. People steal things from each other on every continent, and hate exists in all nations from pole to pole. There is selfishness in Australia, Antarctica and the Americas. Violence is common in faraway wars and in local high schools. All around the world and inside my own heart, I get the sense that there is something very wrong and Genesis 3 points me to its origin.

I am so thankful for the fact that the Bible gives me answers as to why we see all these problems. The Bible says that the world started off as a masterpiece made by a skilled Creator. Then we turned on Him and wanted to go our own way. Now we have to deal with the consequences of that choice.

This is where people start to get a little squirmy.

A Few Words About Hell

Televangelists, the white haired preachers on late night TV, and right-wing fundamentalists were perhaps just a little too brash in presenting the doctrine of sin and hell to our culture. They spoke condescendingly and angrily of a wrathful God who takes delight in sending people to Hell to pay for their many sins where they suffer eternally. Though their message was partially correct, their presentation turned a lot of people away from the church, the Bible, Jesus and Christianity. The damage was so severe that these people literally scared *the Hell* right out of the church — perhaps a reason why no one wants to talk about it anymore.

So what is Hell? It is place reserved for God's eternal punishment for the devil and those who commit sin[38]. In today's culture, talking about Hell is quite taboo; there is no tolerance for an "intolerable" message like the doctrine of Hell. Bringing up the subject will earn you the same "high praise" that you might expect if Oscar Meyer ran for mayor in a vegan colony. Even *Christians* do not want to talk about Hell anymore. Even worse, they do not believe that God would send people to a place where the unrepentant sinners experience what Scripture describes as "conscious and eternal punishment."

I have this problem where I have to tell the truth even when it gets me into trouble. If you are a part of church culture long enough, you will find more and more leaders, authors and bloggers who want to deny the fact that God could send anyone to Hell. The belief they are championing is called Universalism. It is an idea that "everyone is in"- everyone goes to heaven one day. This nice sounding idea is akin to the belief in unicorns, Easter bunnies and tooth fairies; sadly, not unlike the aforementioned mythical creatures, it is not in the Bible and was condemned as heresy (a false belief about God) many years ago. The Universalists of our day come across being very nice people;

---

[38] See Revelation 20-21

unfortunately, their niceness causes them to ignore certain passages, if not entire books, of the Bible. Instead, they create a different set of beliefs that they would rather believe in.

Call me old fashioned, but I don't think you can remove some of Jesus' teachings, as well as the subsequent scriptural doctrines that originate out of those teachings, and still call yourself a follower of this same Jesus. I may give all sorts of claims to being an environmentalist, but if I continue to forget to recycle, drive my gas guzzler, and ignore the teachings of David Suzuki, then I am no environmentalist at all.

I used to think that not believing in Hell was a new problem that our century had created in the name of postmodern tolerance and niceness. Looking into it further, I discovered that this is a very old problem, it just wears a different dress.

St. Augustine Vs. Pelagian Heresy

St. Augustine lived from 354 to 430 AD and is regarded as one of the greatest Christian theologians. Augustine was a real rebel and led a pretty wild life until he had his own epiphany with Jesus. He knew firsthand about sin; a real expert! Augustine believed that all people, as descendants of Adam and Eve, were born with the fatal disease called "original sin." One verse that supports Augustine's belief is found in Ephesians 2:1–2,

"As for you, you were dead in your transgressions and sins, in which you used to live when you followed the ways of this world[39]."

This verse talks about how we are born alive in body but dead in spirit since we are cursed by the "original sin." Because we are born sinful, we merely act out of this nature and go on sinning. Left on our own, we will continue to live and die

---

[39] Ephesians 2:1

in sin in order to pay the price for our rebellion against God. Augustine's greatest opponent to the doctrine of original sin was a man named Pelagius who believed that everyone is born good rather than sinful. This formed the basis for Universalism — if everybody is essentially good, then there is no need to be saved from sin. But, as we discussed earlier, and I hope you agree, there is still sin in our world; we all have the painful wounds to prove it. Augustine fought Pelagius and his followers on this issue, and eventually Pelagius was condemned as a heretic (or "false teacher") in the council of Carthage in May 418 AD.

Although Pelagianism was condemned, the idea of Universalism never really went away. Many hundreds of years later, Charles Haddon Spurgeon, arguably one of the best preachers to ever walk the earth, resisted the pressure to avoid the topic of Hell in his sermons. According to Spurgeon, those who had preceded him were a little too angry, preachy and brash when it came to preaching the dark side of the gospel, namely, Hell. The great preacher explains,

> "Perhaps some of the Puritan fathers may have gone too far, and have given too great a prominence to the terrors of the Lord in their ministry; but the age in which we live has sought to forget those terrors altogether, and if we dare to tell men that God will punish them for their sins, it is charged upon us that we want to bully them into religion, and if we faithfully and honestly tell our hearers that sin must bring after it certain destruction, it is said that we are trying to frighten them into goodness. Now we care not what men mockingly impute to us; we feel it is our duty, when men sin, to tell them that they shall be punished; and so long as the world will not give up its sin, we feel we must not cease our warnings[40]."

---

[40] Spurgeon, Charles H., *Spurgeon's Sermons* (Baker Books, 2007) Volume 2.

Spurgeon suggests that regardless of what injustices others have done, it is our duty to teach people that there is a consequence for their sin today and forever.

G.K. Chesterton has said, "the depravity of man is at once the most empirically verifiable and intellectually resisted argument that we face." Chesterton is telling us that despite all our well intentioned claims about human beings being naturally good, those claims get shot down instantly with any sort of field research as one studies history or the world today. It's all around us but nobody wants to accept it.

You might say this sort of language is just a little too strong, "But… aren't we all just a *little* bit good?" No, we are not good. The only good part in us is the divine image that God has lovingly put in each human being when He made us. The *imago dei*[41] (image of God) gives us all value and dignity as humans. Divine royalty marked us but we are also marred by sin. It wrecked everything. Sin has affected the entire human race so that no one, past, present or future, can ever meet God based on his or her own merit. This idea is what the theologians call "Total Depravity." Here's a great example from Genesis 6:5, "The Lord saw how great man's wickedness on the earth had become and that every inclination of the thoughts of his heart was only evil all the time." We are wicked and we rebel all the time. Every now and then? No, all the time. Without the miracle of His grace, we will only continue to do what we want to do — reject God and follow our sin nature. In this light, Romans 3 starts to make sense.

> "There is no one who understands, no one who seeks God. All have turned away, they have together become worthless; there is no one who does good, not even one[42]."

---

41 Genesis 1:27
42 Romans 3:11-12

Because of original sin, no one is good. Not me, not you, not Oprah, not Gandhi, not anyone. In thought, word and deed, we have all disobeyed the perfect Creator, the Lawgiver and the King of all kings. Left in this state, you and I should die and be forced to pay the full penalty for our sin alone in the place the Bible calls Hell.

That is what we deserve. I understand why no one wants to talk about it. Friends will talk about it though, true friends at least. That's why I'm here for you.

Real Friends Talk About Hell

If I'm hanging out eating wings with some buddies and I get a piece of skin stuck in my teeth, I would hope that my friends would tell me about it. No matter how awkward or uncomfortable it makes me feel, I would hope that someone would tell me that I have something in my teeth. The more someone cares about me, the more prone they are to speak the truth — even if it could hurt or offend me.

We have to talk about Hell because we have to come to terms with the true state of the human condition apart from God. The prophet Jeremiah said that the human heart is deceitful and desperately wicked[43]. Unless we come to understand our utterly hopeless and guilty state without Jesus, we will never understand the importance of what Jesus did for us and, in the process, we will deny the most important event in history — the cross.

If you do not believe in Hell, then everything Jesus did for you on the cross was a waste of His time. Mel Gibson's graphic portrayal of the crucifixion in his movie *The Passion of Christ* really struck a chord with viewers. I don't know about you, but I don't want to be the one to stare Jesus in the face and tell

---

[43]   Jeremiah 17:9

him that he really went through all that intense suffering for nothing.

Those who truly understand the depraved human condition and the sacrifice that Jesus made should be the most passionate worshippers, the most in love with Jesus, and the most thankful for the undeserved grace of God. Jesus told us that those people who understand how much they have been forgiven are the ones who love the strongest.

Does Anyone Have A Better Idea?

The truth is that people want to criticize God about the doctrine of Hell but no one can ever come up with a better idea. Every idea man has imagined portrays a God who is either less loving, less accepting or less tolerant than the God that the Bible teaches us about. So let's talk about some arguments that many people have regarding the doctrine of Hell[44].

Critique #1 — *If God sends people to Hell, then that makes God cruel.*

First, let's make it clear; God does not send people to Hell. Hell is self-selected. God gave Adam and Eve a choice to worship him or reject Him. They chose to reject him and we, their sons and daughters, have followed in their footsteps. I previously mentioned how sin breaks our relationship with God. When I sin, I am walking away from the life and relationship that I know God wants for me and with me. This didn't happen by accident. It is my choice.

Do you remember when you were a kid an aunt who just loved to make you uncomfortable with her awkward sloppy kisses?

---

[44] I owe a great gratitude to my Facebook friend, Mark Driscoll for his help in one of the greatest sermons I have ever heard preached. *Kingdom: God Reigns.* It is available online at *(www. marshillchurch.org)*

Most of us had at least one.l It became something of a tradition at Thanksgiving, Christmas and Easter. You'd walk in the door to a family dinner and be smothered with an unquenchable love that left lip shaped lipstick smears all over you. Multiplied over the years, this terrible experience can make family dinners rather undesirable and counseling rather probable. God is not like your annoying aunt. He will never force a relationship on you or force you to love Him. God is a gentleman. He gives us a choice to accept or reject His invitation of relationship. Knowing humanity's natural desire to reject God, it should come as no surprise that people naturally choose Hell over knowing and being fully known by God.

If some people spent their entire lives hating and rejecting God's offer of love and grace, why would they want to spend eternity in heaven with Him? Heaven, in a way, will be like Hell for them. You may recall the collective groan coming from your classmates and yourself when a teacher turned the lights back on after a video in class. You probably scrambled to cover your eyes when the light attacked your pupils. The light was unexpected and unwelcome because your eyes had grown so accustomed to darkness. It hurt. Now think about what it would be like if you lived your entire life in the dark. Seeing a great light, in fact the brightest light of all would be a very terrible, painful experience. The book of John talks about how Jesus is the light of the world but men reject the light because they love darkness instead[45]. People that love darkness want nothing to do with light and God is kind enough to let them stay in the dark, as they so desire.

In my opinion, C.S. Lewis sums this idea up perfectly with a wise observation, "There are those who say to God, 'Thy will be done' and those to whom God says (on the final day), 'Thy will be done[46]."

---

[45]   John 3:19

[46]   Lewis, C.S. The Great Divorce, (HarperCollins, 1973).

For those who choose to walk in light, however, God is willing to accept anyone including the worst of sinners. History is full of great stories where repentant tyrants, criminals, murderers, child pornographers, prostitutes, and Bible College students choose to follow Christ and find freedom from guilt, shame, greed, themselves and Hell.

Critique #2 — *Hell Makes God Intolerant*

Everyone is a fundamentalist on at least one topic. If you do not believe me, head over to Vancouver Island, find a hippy in an artsy community and tell them that you think Mother Nature is a prostitute. Tell them how you think recycling wastes taxpayer money and how you would much rather have that money back in your wallet to pay for the gas that your SUV consumes. Oh yes and before you leave, mention how you feel it is your civic duty to speed up Global Warming because you look forward to making the cold Canadian winters a little more bearable.

I wonder how they would react to your point of view. Their reaction would most certainly be intolerant to your views, which doesn't seem right. How dare those tree-hugging hippies kick you out of their community? What right do they have to make judgments about your lifestyle choices?

The truth is that those Island-dwelling tie-dye enthusiasts would have every right to kick you out of their community. In their minds, you would be wrecking everything — destroying the earth, yourself and those around you in the process.

If God is intolerant, it is because he does not want sinners ruining everything that He has created. Rapists need to stop raping and murderers need to stop murdering. Pedophiles, cheaters, adulterers, and pornographers, cannot be tolerated in God's perfect community. Should these people be allowed to continue to carry out their destructive acts forever? Is that the kind of world that you want in the name of tolerance?

71

"No, no, no, just the good people should go to heaven," you might say. But it is a very intolerant thing to suggest that you can be the judge of calling some people good and some not good.

Here's a word of advice: don't be fooled! The people who are the strongest supporters of tolerance in the world are often the most intolerant. If you don't share the same views as they do, you are probably not going to get an invite to dinner. That is intolerance if you ask me. Ironic isn't it?

So who then draws the line in the sand to say who's good and bad? If we're honest, the "good" people are those who are most like us, agree with us, and who have found favour in our minds. If we're honest, we would all like to be the judges of who is in and who is out. Fortunately, God never offered us this position. Again, remember what the Bible says, there are no "good" people.

"All have sinned and fallen short of the glory of God[47]."

The fact that God even allows *anyone* into heaven is a miracle, and it is only because of what Jesus did on the cross that we can ask forgiveness and follow Him. Because of this, our God should be celebrated for being the most tolerant God that we could possible imagine. Personally, I am thankful for His tolerance as it allows you and me the opportunity to enter into a relationship with Him. "He is patient with you, not wanting anyone to perish, but everyone to come to repentance[48]."

Critique #3 — *Hell Makes God Unloving*

I guess the problem with talking about love is that we really have no idea what love is at all. We say, "I love steak!" or "I love the Vancouver Canucks!" But what does this mean? Our current construct of love seems quite subjective if you ask me.

---

[47] Romans 3:23
[48] 2 Peter 3:9

What if the steak was old and the Canucks were never to win a Stanley Cup? (Lord forbid!) Would I still say I love them? Based on this idea, here are some questions to consider. Do you really love anything in the truest sense of the word? Do we even have a true definition of love apart from what the Bible teaches? Can you admit that, for your entire life, media and culture has bombarded you with lies about the reality of love? Would you be willing to admit that you may have no idea what real love is or how God, the Creator of love, loves us in a real way[49]?

When I say that I love my friends and family, I believe that I genuinely love them the best I possibly can. If someone were to warn me that a family member or one of my friends was going to be hurt, I would probably do my best to prevent that from happening. What if I did not stop them? What if great harm was inflicted upon my loved ones and I did nothing?

Thankfully, we have a justice system that ensures that I do not have to take matters into my own hands. Violent people are locked up and forced to pay for their crimes against humanity, disallowing continued violent behavior. Sometimes the crime is so harsh that the criminal is imprisoned for their entire lives. Death is a boundary that keeps criminals from continuing to hurt people forever.

Can you imagine if we had no system to punish criminals, and they were allowed to continue committing crimes over and over again? Can you imagine if they didn't die and kept it up for eternity?

It is nice to sit in our comfy suburban homes and think of a God who would never punish anyone for sin. This seems to fit well into our culture's idealistic perspective on God and the "goodness" of the world. I ask you, however, what about those who took machetes to almost one million innocent Tutsis in Rwanda during the genocide of 1994? What about the Nazis who smashed babies like baseball bats against walls to kill them faster? What if the people, who committed these

---

[49]   1 John 4:9

unspeakable crimes, were allowed to do this for eternity without consequence? Would a loving God really allow this to happen forever? The thought is absurd.

I go crazy thinking about all the injustice that goes on in the world, and I'm thankful that God takes care of seeing it through so I do not have to. I want to see evil punished and justice served. God is much more loving than you or I because He always gives sinners a way out.

We see the great love of God as He allows Jesus to take the punishment for the sins we committed. On the cross, humanity's curse of original sin is diverted to Jesus so that even the worst criminals are able to find mercy and grace when they really deserve the punishment of death[50].

If you do choose to reject this ultimate act of love done by Jesus on your behalf, you are left with nothing[51]. You must pay for your offenses against God even though He has taken every measure to ensure that this does not have to happen. Rather than literally arguing yourself to death and ultimately finding your position untenable, you would do best to repent of your sin and avoid it.

> "Christ died for the ungodly. Very rarely will anyone die for a righteous man, though for a good man someone might possibly dare to die. But God demonstrates his own love for us in this: while we were still sinners, Christ died for us[52]."

Critique #4 — *If God created everything and Hell is where God is not, then how could Hell be a real place?*

This is a long discussion. I would point you to several places for answers to this one: C.S. Lewis, Charles Haddon Spurgeon, and

---

[50]   1 Corinthians 5:21
[51]   1 John 4:8
[52]   Romans 5:7-8

John Piper as well as many others that have written volumes on this topic. I will quickly clear a misconception about God which might help answer this critique, especially to those who adhere to a heresy called, annihilationism. I will start with a quote from Spurgeon, "But it is the cry of the age that God is merciful, that God is love. Ay, who said he was not? But remember, it is equally true, God is just, severely and inflexibly just!"

As was already discussed, God is love. God is also just. He has been wronged by our sin. We broke His rules. Sin has been committed and God lets us know from cover to cover in the Bible that He does not tolerate sin. Without Jesus, we are left in our sin and destined to be punished.

There are some who claim that Hell could not exist because they falsely believe that God cannot have any part of Hell. Revelation 14:10 shows us that God's enemies will be tormented in the presence of all the angels and the Lamb, Jesus.

How could Jesus stand such a sight you might ask? I believe that in as much as God is glorified when someone receives grace and salvation from sin, so too is justice carried out when unrepentant sinners receive punishment for their disobedience. God shows that He is just and true when people receive the eternal consequences of their rebellion. Satan and the demons are punished as surely as those who belong to them. We are eternal beings, intended for an eternal relationship with our Creator but the choice of where we spend eternity is ours. Everyone lives forever somewhere and God will be glorified no matter where that is.

The Bible says that God is the "Lord of all." All means everything. There is nowhere that Jesus is not Lord.

Even in Hell.

Almost There

There you go. We made it. I had to write about Hell because I know that deep down you can handle it. I also had to tell you this because I love you and want you to avoid Hell at all costs. I am sure you would rather have someone tell you the truth now than to learn it when it is too late. Understanding Hell through a Biblical perspective helps us understand why people behave the way they do. It explains why you do what you should not do, and why you do not do what you should do. It will help you make sense of the fact that some of you, even after being warned, will put down this book and go look at porn, gossip about a friend, have sex with your boyfriend or girlfriend, cheat on a test or _____ (you pick something). You will do this because you are a sinner by nature and deed. This chapter was all about the bad news. The next chapter, however, is full of good news; news about how we can avoid having to bear the penalty that we deserve.

To truly appreciate the sweet, you often need to taste the bitter first.

The next chapter is going to be so very sweet indeed.

The Gospel

The Right Dying So The Wrong Can Be Made Right

"The gospel to me is simply irresistible"
-Blaise Pascal

If there were only one thing you could talk about for the rest of your life, what would it be? If there were one sermon I could preach for the rest of my time on earth, I would preach this one. I am very excited to write out my favourite story in the whole world — God's redemption story. At the same time, I am very humbled to know that no matter what I type, it will never do justice to just how great the content matter is.

There is nothing I could say that could come close to equalling the good news of Jesus.

No words that I could join together could ever compare with the eloquence of God's grace. The greatest minds and writers of all time could not cover the absolute greatness that is found in the gospel of Jesus. If you only read one chapter in this book, read this one.

Martin Luther, the fiery German who led the Protestant Reformation in the sixteenth century, taught his apprentices: "The truth of the gospel is the principle article of Christian doctrine. Most necessary is it that we must know it well and teach it to others and beat it into their heads constantly."

More than anything, Luther wanted Christians to know the gospel story. So passionate was his desire that beating it into people was acceptable behaviour. This will be the most beneficial beating you have ever received. No matter where you stand with Jesus, you will, by the end of this chapter, know what He has done for you and why the Christians think He is such a big deal. The beatings shall begin with the famous Bible verse found in John 3:16.

> "For God so loved the world that he gave his one and only Son that whoever believes in him should not perish but have eternal life[53]."

You may have seen this verse posted in all sorts of places: at sporting events, on bumper stickers and, to the very bold, as tattoos. There is a reason why this verse is so popular. It tells our story. It gives us hope that there is a way to avoid the judgment of God, punishment for sin, spiritual death and eternity in hell. Though we certainly deserve all these things, God in His grace and mercy had another idea to rescue His creation.

A Lesson From A Rebellious Puck Stopper

In hockey, if you are going to be a goalie, you have to be a bit different. It's an entirely different game from what all the other players experience; you have a different helmet, different pads, different stick and different gloves. You're out there all by yourself with no one to talk to but yourself. There is also a lot of

---

[53] John 3:16

pressure for a goalie. Goalies know, regardless of whether or not anyone else agrees with them, that the difference between a win, lose, or championship all depends on how well the goalie plays.

Hockey players know the importance of their last line of defense, and so they learn to tolerate their goalie despite his or her "differentness." Besides, someone has to be intellectually inept enough to stand in front of high-speed, flying rubber pucks and take them in the most sensitive of places. I seemed to fit that criterion well, and therefore I played the entirety of my competitive hockey career as a goalie.

Due to the fact that goalies are so important and rare, there is a certain amount of assumed respect for what they do and an effort to maintain their protection. All hockey players know that an opposing player is not to enter the other goalie's crease. It is forbidden ground and failure to respect a goalie's crease results in strict consequences. When a player happened to enter *my* crease, I found that a punch to the back of the neck with the blocker to be an effective communicative tool to make him aware of his unwelcome presence. Sometimes it was a slash behind the knee or a slew foot (kicking the back of their skates sending the players up into the air and onto their hind quarters) that would be the final straw to send my foe to the hard ice and out of my personal bubble.

The only problem with these malicious but effective tactics is that you're not allowed to do them. Committing these infractions is considered breaking the rules of hockey. It is forbidden for a goalie to punch players in the head, slash them behind the knees or slew foot them to the ground. If you are new to the sport of hockey or have never cared about hockey before this moment, you need to know that when you break the rules, you get a penalty. An offence has happened, the rules have been broken and a price must be paid for it. You are sent to the "sin bin," hockey's version of Hell, also popularly termed "the penalty box."

Any referee worth his weight in salt will not overlook such an infraction. The cool thing is that though I took all these penalties for my many acts of violence toward my foes, I never sat in the penalty box once. When a goalie gets a penalty, another player has to serve the penalty in his stead so that the goalie can stay in the game. I will return to this illustration soon, but for now let's return to our first parents in the Garden of Eden.

From Genesis To Revelation: God's Plan Of Restoration

Adam and Eve broke God's one rule. "Thou shall not eateth from this specific tree." They ateth, of course, and as a result all hell broke loose on earth. Thankfully, all was not lost. God had a plan.

For God so loved the world.

In Genesis 3:15 God, after cursing the serpent for his deception of Adam and Eve, gives us a sneak peak at how He will put back together the broken relationship with humanity — His most precious and beloved creation. Though we screw up and run from God, it is great to know that He will always provide a way back to Him. The restoration promise looks like this,

"I will put enmity between you and the woman and between your offspring and hers; he will crush your head and you will strike his heel[54]."

I will give you a good ten dollar word that is sure to impress everyone during your first year of Bible School (don't use it in real school or you will get made fun of). It comes in reference

---

[54]   Genesis 3:15

to Genesis 3:15 when God shows His plan to reverse the consequences of sin. The word is:

Protoevangelium.

Literally the "first good news." According to this passage, there will come a day when one will be born of a woman who will be different from all the other babies in history. This baby would grow up with a fight on his hands. He will deal a deathblow to the serpent (Satan) and yet suffer heavily because of it.

It is encouraging to know that on our most tragic day as humans here in Genesis 3, God shows that He does not give up on us. Though full of anger and heartbreak over humanity's choice to reject His love invitation, God says, "There will come a day in history when I will end this curse of sin forever. However, it will come at a great cost to me."

The next sections will show how God carries out this plan starting with a sacrificial system for the Jewish people, and then a sacrifice by God Himself for the whole world.

The Lamb

In case you haven't seen the movie, *Prince Of Egypt*, let me get you up to date with the story. God raised up a leader named Moses, who led the mass exit, or *exodus*, of the Jewish people out of Pharaoh's oppression. Of course, Pharaoh was not so cool with having his highly organized slave operation crumble, and resisted letting the Jews go free. God insisted and sent ten plagues to the Egyptians to show that the God of the Israelites was more powerful than Egypt's gods and Egypt's ruler. So the rivers turned to blood, which is gross unless you enjoy Clamato juice, as well as infestations of flies, gnats and locusts just to name a few. The final judgment or the last plague on Egypt was where the Jewish people got the celebration that they still celebrate today called the Passover.

The first Passover came when God told Moses to instruct the people to slaughter one lamb per family and to smear the blood of the lamb on the doorposts[55]. When the angel of death passed by that night, he saw the blood and "passed over" that house, sparing that family's firstborn son from death. The firstborn son represented a lot in those days. He was the bloodline — the one who would keep the family name going. He was the future of the family. Without the blood on their doors, the Egyptian firstborn boys died that night.

God was saying to Pharaoh and all of Egypt that refusing to acknowledge and submit to Him as the true God would result in the destruction of you and your bloodline. While it sounds tough, Pharaoh had to play by God's rules.

An innocent lamb was killed and its blood was used to save the Jewish people from death.

The Sacrificial System Pointing To An Ultimate Sacrifice

Later on in the Jewish sacrificial system (the Law), a slaughtered lamb was considered a ransom that had to be paid to release people from the judgment of their sin. A man would bring a lamb to the temple and its sacrifice would be sufficient in God's eyes as payment for the man's sins. This was good news for a sinful, rebellious people who wanted to be forgiven for their sins. It is not really good news for the lambs.

The lamb was killed so that a person didn't have to be. This is the idea that theologians call *substitutionary atonement*. Substitutionary means, "to take the place of" and atonement means, "satisfaction for a wrong or injury."

Many years later, God told Isaiah, a prophet of God, something very interesting. That's what good prophets do; they hear

---

[55] Exodus 12:21

from God and then say it out loud — no matter how weird it sometimes sounds.

In Isaiah 53, he said that one day God will walk on the earth and will give up His life for the forgiveness of the world's sin. He will be like "a lamb that is led to the slaughter[56]." Isaiah is saying that a day is coming when God will be like a Passover Lamb, the ultimate sacrifice once and for all.

One day a lamb will come but it will be no ordinary lamb. This lamb will be God himself. This lamb will also be a man.

A Much Anticipated, Unprecedented Birth

Scholars say that there are over 300 prophecies about the coming of Jesus in the Bible, including where He would be born, how He would live and how he would die. The Israelites eagerly looked forward to the coming of the Messiah who would preach good news to the poor, mend broken hearts, and proclaim freedom for those in captivity to their sin[57].

Four hundred years later in the town of Bethlehem[58], a region of Galilee[59], a baby boy born of a virgin entered the world and was named Jesus. The one who created the world was now in the world. This is what we call "the incarnation," from the Latin "*incarnatione*[60]" (literally "in meat").

God came in meat. Jesus showed up just as Isaiah and the other prophets said that He would. The one who would deliver the people from sin, preach good news to the poor, bind up

---

[56]   Isaiah 53:7
[57]   Isaiah 61:1
[58]   Micah 5:1
[59]   Isaiah 9:1
[60]   Kudos to Mark Driscoll for help on this one. Taken from Doctrine: God Comes (*www.marshillchurch.org/media/doctrine/ incarnation-god-comes*)

the broken hearted and proclaim freedom for the captives was finally here. It blows my mind to reflect on this truth. The Creator of the universe, the eternal timeless One stepped into the limitations of time to breathe our air, bathe in our water, and even have His diapers changed.

People were excited to see Jesus, the God-man. He drew a crowd wherever He went. This is why when Jesus steps onto the scene in the first chapter of John's gospel, John the Baptist, His cousin, announces to the crowd, "Behold, the lamb of God who takes away the sins of the world[61]." He's saying, "Here is the one that was promised long ago. Here is the Lamb we've all been waiting for! The future is now! The kingdom of God is finally here."

Jesus steps onto the scene and starts showing people what things are like in God's kingdom. He showed the world a different way to live. His ministry was to those the world had ignored: the poor, the sick, the beggars, the prostitutes, the outcasts, and the kid that nobody wants to be friends with because he doesn't shower, dresses in a trenchcoat and always wants to talk about online video games. Those are the people Jesus helped most. He loved to heal them, to hang out with them, to show them that though no one else may care, God does.

"It is not the healthy that need a doctor but the sick[62]."

He was called a friend of sinners[63]. I bet Jesus was really fun to hang out with. He got invited to parties, and was always accused by religious people of being a drunk and eating too much food when he was out with people.

---

[61]   John 1:29
[62]   Mark 2:17, Luke 5:31
[63]   Matthew 11:19

A Different Kind Of Teacher

It wasn't the people that Jesus hung out with that made him different; it was also what he talked about that shook everything up. In a culture where the rich and powerful seemed to be the best of the blessed, Jesus turned that whole thinking upside down and said,

"No, no, blessed are the poor in Spirit, those whose only hope is in God."

The culture said, "Blessed are the ones who do great in battle."
Jesus said, "No, no, blessed are the peacemakers."
You are blessed when you give rather than take.
You are blessed if you seek to serve rather than to be served.
You are blessed if you're willing to be last in line and not always wanting to be first.
You truly live when you die to yourself[64].

No doubt about it, the guy was radical.

It is no wonder that people thought he was a great teacher. He said a lot of revolutionary things that no one else was teaching at the time. Many throughout history, regardless of whether or not they called themselves Christians, have respected Jesus' teachings. The problem with this is that Jesus will not allow you to cap Him off as merely a teacher. As C.S. Lewis explains, we cannot call Jesus solely a good teacher because He claimed to be so much more than that. Jesus said he was God.

> "I am trying here to prevent anyone saying the really foolish thing that people often say about Him: "I'm ready to accept Jesus as a great moral teacher, but I don't accept His claim to be God." That is the one thing we must not say. A man who said the sort of things Jesus said would not be a great moral teacher. He would either

---

[64]   See the Sermon On The Mount Matthew 5-7

be a lunatic — on a level with the man who says he is a poached egg — or else he would be the Devil of Hell. You must make your choice. Either this man was, and is, the Son of God: or else a madman or something worse. You can shut Him up for a fool, you can spit at Him and kill Him as a demon; or you can fall at His feet and call Him Lord and God. But let us not come with any patronizing nonsense about His being a great human teacher. He has not left that open to us. He did not intend to[65]."

Not many great teachers claim to be God like Jesus did. In claiming to be God, he has given us two choices: either we believe he is who he said he is or he is nuts. If a guy walked into your school or your work and made the kind of claims that Jesus did, you would look at getting the guy locked up in a protective room so he wouldn't hurt himself.

The Mission Of Jesus

We need to understand that Jesus was God because it sets us up for the third objective. It was not just about the ministry or the message but the mission. Jesus said, "I have come to seek and save the lost[66]." John later states, "The reason the Son of God appeared was to destroy the devil's work[67]."

Jesus came as a fulfillment of the protoevangelium promise of Genesis 3:15. He came to reverse the curse of sin in the world and pay the great price that doing so would entail.

Isaiah prophesied in chapter 53 what that price would look like for God's chosen one,

---

[65]   Lewis, C.S. Mere Christianity (HarperCollins, 1952). Page 52.
[66]   Luke 19:10
[67]   1 John 3:8

"But he was pierced for our transgressions, he was crushed for our iniquities; the punishment that brought us peace was upon him, and by his wounds we are healed[68]."

The chosen one would be pierced, crushed, punished, and later it says that he would suffer to the point of his own death. He, who lived a sinless life, would suffer a criminal's death as a sacrifice on behalf of the guilty[69]. Remember, this was written 700 years before the crucifixion of Jesus. It's astounding.

There is Jesus, walking with His disciples, telling them all these great truths about what God's kingdom is like. Every once in awhile, He would drop a bomb about how He would have to suffer greatly and die in obedience to accomplish what He had been sent to do.

Nobody believed him, but he kept talking about it anyway. Then one day after dinner as the Jews were all celebrating the annual Passover meal — the celebration of the Passover lamb when God delivered them from Egypt — Jesus was approached by a group of men who had come to arrest Him and would eventually hand Him over to be killed. The next day he was tried as a criminal and sentenced to death by crucifixion — one of the most painful and humiliating ways to die. Crucifixion is so painful that the word excruciating comes from its Latin root "to crucify[70]."

This was what Jesus did for us. The one who was foretold from long ago, who came preaching a message of God's love for the broken, hurting, poor, outcast, and forgotten, was hung on a cross by the very people whom He came to save.

---

[68] Isaiah 53:6

[69] Isaiah 53:9

[70] excruciating. (n.d.). *Dictionary.com Unabridged (v 1.1)*. Retrieved March 17, 2009, from Dictionary.com

On the other hand, Jesus put Himself on the cross. Jesus told us that He was not forced or strong armed into death on a cross; it was an endeavor He took on willingly.

"The reason my Father loves me is that I lay down my life — only to take it up again. No one takes it from me, but I lay it down of my own accord. I have authority to lay it down and authority to take it up again[71]."

"Why did Jesus have to die?" you might ask. Jesus laid down his life as adequate payment to satisfy the demands of God's holiness. Another ten dollar word the Bible uses to describe this is, "propitiation" or "that which satisfies." By Christ's death on the cross, the offense of our sin against God was paid for in full. The Bible describes Jesus as the mediator, the one who bridges the gap between us and God that we cannot hope to fix on our own. "There is one God, and there is one mediator between God and men, the man Christ Jesus who gave himself as a ransom" (1 Tim. 2:5–6). Jesus was fully God as well as fully human but without sin. He experienced the complete human existence and so was the perfect bridge.

This is huge. In fact, it is so enormous that it would be unwise to move on without hitting the point home just one more time regarding what Jesus did for us on the cross.

In 2 Corinthians 5:21, Paul writes, "God made him who knew no sin to be sin for us that we might become the righteousness of God." Do you see what Paul is saying here? The first part talks about Jesus becoming sin for us. God puts all of the punishment for our sins, our mistakes, our rebellion, our greed, our pride from the past, present and future, onto Jesus. Instead of Jon Morrison carrying his own sins, Jesus willingly bears them for him.

---

[71] John 10:17-18

And then there's the second half of that great 2 Corinthians verse, "that we might be called the righteousness of God[72]." After placing our sin on Christ, God then takes the pure and sinless righteousness of Jesus and puts it onto us. We are no longer dirty with our sin. We are seen as pure, white and holy. "For on this day shall atonement be made for you to cleanse you. You shall be clean before the Lord from all your sins[73]." When God looks at us now, He sees the clean, pure, innocent Jesus!

Martin Luther calls this, "The Great Exchange" and what a great exchange it is! Christ takes our sin and we get His righteousness. How is that fair? It's not fair, but that's Jesus. This is why so many Christian songs talk about God's grace being amazing. I mean sure, you'd think these professional artists could come up with some new words other than just "amazing" but maybe they don't have to. That's what God's grace is: amazing.

Then comes the best news — the lynchpin in the story. Christ was not held down by sin. Sin and death do not get the last word. After lying there dead for three days, the Bible teaches that Jesus came back to life. He conquered death. Sin has officially been defeated through Jesus. The curse of Genesis 3 has been reversed and humanity's relationship with God is officially restored.

Here's Colossians 2:14 as paraphrased in The Message,

> "God brought you alive — right along with Christ! Think of it! All sins forgiven, the slate wiped clean, that old arrest warrant canceled and nailed to Christ's cross. He stripped all the spiritual tyrants in the universe of their sham authority at the Cross and marched them naked through the streets."

---

[72]   2 Corinthians 5:21
[73]   Leviticus 16:30

Those who would choose to believe this and follow the Lord Jesus, experience victory over humanity's second greatest fear — death.

> "Where, O death, is your victory? Where, O death, is your sting? The sting of death is sin, and the power of sin is the law. But thanks be to God! He gives us the victory through our Lord Jesus Christ[74]."

Is it not the greatest moment in *The Lion, The Witch And The Wardrobe* when Lucy and Susan look back at the Stone Table thinking they will catch one last look at a murdered Aslan only to see that the great lion is gone? Aslan appears again standing right there beside them alive and well.

> [Lucy and Susan] looked around. There, shining in the sunrise, larger than they had seen him before, shaking his mane stood Aslan himself.
> "Aren't you dead then, dear Aslan?" said Lucy.
> "Not now," said Aslan...
> "But what does it all mean?" asked Susan when they were somewhat calmer.
> "It means, said Aslan, "that though the Witch knew the Deep Magic, there is a magic deeper still which she did not know. Her knowledge goes back only to the dawn of time. If she could have looked further back... she would have known that when a willing victim who had committed no treachery was killed in a traitor's stead, the Table would crack and Death itself would start working backwards[75]."

Aslan paid the penalty of death demanded for the traitorous actions of Edmund. Jesus has done the same for traitors like you and I. It is not enough that Jesus defeats death with his

---

[74] 1 Corinthians 15:55-56
[75] Lewis, C.S. *The Lion, The Witch and The Wardrobe*. (Harper-Collins, 1950). Page 152.

resurrection; there is one final act in this story to mention. That is, when He wraps it all up in the end, a day we eagerly await.

Revelation: The Last Word

In Revelation, the final book in the Bible, Jesus is seen triumphing over His enemies and His relationship with His people is fully restored in a great celebration in Heaven. If you love Jesus and He is the leader of your life, you can have hope that when all the smoke is cleared, when the guns of centuries of war have been silenced, when all the school papers and pages of human history have been written, you can have confidence that you are on the winning team. At the end of the Bible, Jesus emerges as the hero of world history and the cool thing is that we even get to hang out with Him.

> "Then I saw a new heaven and a new earth, for the first heaven and the first earth had passed away and there was no longer any sea (a biblical symbol for sin and chaos). I saw the Holy City, the New Jerusalem, coming down out of heaven from God, prepared as a bride beautifully dressed for her husband. And I heard a loud voice from the throne saying "Now the dwelling place of God is with men and he will live with them. They will be his people and God himself will be with them and be their God. He will wipe every tear from their eyes. There will be no more death or mourning or crying or pain, for the old order of things has passed away[76]."

Sin and all its effects are forever gone. Jesus has gotten rid of them and is united with His people in a great wedding celebration. God's saving plan from the time of Genesis 3 until now will find its fulfillment on this day in Revelation 21. What a great day it will be to fall down at the feet of the crowned King Jesus, the hero, and do nothing but worship.

---

[76] Revelation 21:1–4

So What?

That is the Gospel story. Congratulations, you have made it through one of the most intensely theological chapters of this book. It gets easier from here but certainly not less important. If all those things about Heaven and Hell are true, you have some deciding to do.

Receive Freedom In Christ

If you are not a Christian, if you have never surrendered your sinfulness and your life to Jesus and wish to do so, then there is no better time than right now. If you have realized you are a sinner and that without a Savior you will spend your eternity separated from God, then you can receive Jesus' free gift right now.

Here's a prayer you can say:

> "Dear Jesus, I am sorry for all the things I have done wrong in my life (take a few minutes here to ask His forgiveness for anything in particular that is on your conscience.) Pelase forgive me. I now trun from everything that I know is wrong.
>
> Thank you that you died on the cross for me so that I can be forgiven and set free.
>
> Thank you that you offer me forgiveness and the gift of Your Spirit to live in me. I now receive that gift. Please come into my life by your Holy Spirit to be with me forever. Thank you Lord Jesus, Amen."

If you prayed something like that, you can go to sleep tonight knowing that Jesus has paid the penalty in your stead. Tomorrow morning, you will awake fully understanding Paul's words, "There is now no condemnation for those who are in Christ Jesus[77]."

Rest In His Promises

If you have already given your life to Jesus, you need to rest in some of the promises that God has given to you. Sometimes you may not feel like you are saved from your sin or that God has really forgiven you. Feelings can change but the truth never does. Sometimes the enemy will attack you with negative thoughts that will affect your feelings. If you're *feeling* like your sin has not been forgiven, I would encourage you to continually go back to the one source of unchanging truth that we have, the Bible. You don't fight feelings with feelings; you fight feelings with the truth.

Sometimes the enemy will try to bring old sins back to the forefront of your mind and try to condemn you for them again. To combat this, one night at youth group we had our students write their sins on some paper and bring them to a cross placed at the front. The students then cut the paper into pieces and, on a separate piece of paper wrote, "I was forgiven of _____on _____ and the Bible says that they are remembered no more." I encouraged my students that whenever they feel the enemy's false accusations, to pull out this paper and remember the forgiveness and cleansing that God promises to all who ask. We put this verse at the bottom of their page,

> "If we confess our sins, he is faithful and just to forgive us our sins and cleanse us from all unrighteousness[78]."

I would encourage you to do an exercise like this as well. Also, I think you'll find it helpful in these times of doubt or attack to read and re-read Romans 8, Psalm 103 or Psalm 51. Commit

---

[77] Romans 8:1
[78] 1 John 1:9

certain verses to memory so that they will help you when doubt or discouragement start to overwhelm you.

The forgiveness of Jesus Christ ensures that you no longer have to worry about all the sin from your past being hurled into your present. If it is in the past, it's gone. As Spurgeon says, God has "cast it behind His back forever." If that's how God deals with it, you probably should too. If nothing else, in the words of my friends in New York,

"Fuggedaboudit"

Religion Is For Jerks

Religious people are the ones who think that they can earn God's favour by doing a bunch of good stuff. Donating to the Food Bank is good but a can of peas that have spent two years in your parent's pantry will not pay enough for the hideousness of your sin! I think the reason that Jesus couldn't stand religious people is because they thought they could do what only He could do — make payment for sin. So when religious people fail to live up to God's standards, they get really sad and depressed. When they think that they're doing alright (at least better than others), they stop getting invited to parties. Either way, Jesus came because religion was not enough; it was even destructive.

"It is by grace you have been saved through faith — and this is not from yourselves, it is a gift from God, not by works so that no one can boast[79]."

Do not forget that your forgiveness is a gift by the grace of God. It is nothing that you have done but rather belief and acceptance in what Christ has done for you. Don't think for one second that your "good deeds" are going to get you into good standing with God. The Bible uses very disgusting and graphic

[79]   Ephesians 2:8-9

94

language to describe our Christ-less "good works" in God's presence referring to them as filthy menstral rags in Isaiah[80] and feces in Philipians 3[81]. It's gross, I know. Your attempts at trying to please by "being good" are gross before God and certainly do not earn you good standing with Him.

Jesus alone is the one who makes atonement for our sins —not you. It's not about reading your Bible enough, praying enough or going to Church enough to make God happy with you. Those are good things to help you grow in your faith, but we do them *because* of what Jesus has done for us.

If you are religious, you need to repent of your sin and once again remember that it is by the grace of Jesus Christ alone that you can be forgiven and be seen as righteous in God's sight.

And Back To Hockey...

It all ties back into hockey of course; the best things in life always do. Jesus took the penalty for us so we, the goalies, could stay in the game. Who would have thought that all my years punching, tripping, and slashing players would have been a foretaste of the gospel message, the good news of Jesus — my favourite story in the whole world.

If only I'd known then what I know now it may have been easier to plead my case.

"But Mr. Referee, I'm merely preaching the gospel!"

> "To him who is able to keep you from falling and to present you before his glorious presence without fault

---

[80] Isaiah 64:6 The NIV's interpretation of the Hebrew "beged" is "Filthy rags" but "used tampons" gives a little more punch to the disgust of religious deeds in God's sight...it's gross, I know.

[81] Philipians 3:8. Our modern day translations are too politically correct for this author.

and with great joy to — the only Savior be glory, majesty, power and authority, through Jesus Christ our Lord, before all ages, now and forevermore! Amen[82]."

---

[82]   Jude 1:24

Getting Comfortable With Being Uncomfortable

And Being Forever Changed Because Of It

"Let justice roll on like a mighty river,
righteousness like a never-failing stream!"
Amos 5:24

A smile comes to my face when I think about some of the friends that I have made in these past couple years. Guys like Sam, Jack, Garvin, Brad and Jim bring up a bunch of memories and accompanying smiles to go with those memories. Though I call them my friends, they are not the type of guys I usually hang out with. They are not particularly educated men; they do not have successful careers, houses of their own or any money. These friends of mine live off the generosity of the government welfare system and non-profit organizations provide them with the necessities of living: food, clothing and shelter. My friends have wisdom but it is wisdom that comes with a lot of scars — consequences of poor decisions in their past. They struggle with serious addictions such as alcohol, drugs, sex or stealing. These men, however messed up they may seem, have become my friends and their friendship has changed my thinking, my faith, my bank account, my priorities, and my leisure time — that's quite an impact if you ask me.

This chapter is one long story of how God brought me, a preppy middle class youth pastor, to a place called Potters Place Mission and how it changed my life.

Finding A Story Worth Telling

Here's my problem: I love to be comfortable. I like to have nice things and I like to take naps. I value being well rested, well fed and warm. As much as I enjoy personal comfort, I know that comfortable living equals boring living. I know there is value in discomfort. I love the adventure, passion and excitement that comes with getting uncomfortable.

Remember in the Cool chapter when we talked about how a worthwhile story has a worthwhile objective? Nobody goes to watch a movie about a guy relaxing on his couch, eating chicken wings and watching movies all day. To review, the greatest stories feature main characters who seek to accomplish a great vision, a noble objective worth fighting for, and then give everything they have to see it happen. William Wallace in *Braveheart* fights to see a Scotland that is free from English oppression. William Wilburforce in *Amazing Grace* fights to abolish the dehumanizing practices of the Trans-Atlantic slave trade. Frodo and Sam journey to take a ring to Mordor to rid the world of the Dark Lord Sauron's influence. In these great stories, we identify with the protagonists because we believe some things, no matter how costly, are worth fighting for. The brave men and women in our favourite stories spend their lives fighting for a worthwhile cause and often pay a great price — sometimes giving up their very lives for it.

This is why all these stupid movies about useless womanizing college frat boys who act like hormone enraged idiots are only appreciated by useless womanizing college frat boys looking for justification to behave like hormone enraged idiots. After the cheap laughs and superfluous amount of female skin have subsided, these movies lack any sort of depth of thought or depth of plot. The makers of these films do not care to develop a plot; their target audience can barely even spell "plot."

For the first time in my life, I have a steady career, medical benefits, money in my bank account, food in the fridge and a tank full of gas. On a comfort scale, ten being "Very Comfortable" and one being "Very Uncomfortable," I am around a nine. Nobody wants to see a movie about a guy who scores a nine on this one. It wouldn't even make it on CBC.

By the grace of God I was saved from a life of boredom with a holy kick in the teeth. This is the story of just how hard God's boot had to swing to get me there.

The Day Things Got Interesting

I once took a two-week tour of Israel and absolutely loved it. We floated in the Dead Sea, sailed on the Sea of Galilee, and sat in ancient synagogues where Jesus had undoubtedly visited. It was during my last day in Jerusalem, at the Holocaust museum called "Yad Vashem" when I realized I would have to start getting uncomfortable.

Before we took one step through the museum doors, our guide took time to point out that there were roughly 14,000 trees planted around the perimeter of the museum. Each tree had a name inscribed on a plaque to honour a person who had risked his or her own life to save a Jewish person during the Holocaust.

I saw that Oscar Schindler had his own tree. I guess he made the list.

At first I was impressed that there were 14,000 people who tried to stop the Holocaust from happening. 14,000 is quite a big number. $14,000 for instance, is a lot of money to me. If I owned 14,000 cars, I would have a lot of cars. I interrupted the guide wondering out loud as to why these 14,000 people did not make a greater impact to prevent this evil scar on world history. How did they not stop the death of over six million Jews during WW2 as Adolf Hitler's "Final Solution" to eliminate the Jewish race?

The tour guide was not impressed with my external processing and proceeded to share with the group that of the 350 million Europeans at the time, 14,000 is less than one percent of the population. 14,000 did not seem like such a big number to me anymore.

Years before that, British philosopher Edmund Burke said, "Evil prevails when good men do nothing." In the Holocaust, we see Burke's prophecy fulfilled. Evil prevailed because less than one percent of the people did anything to stop it.

Nobody did anything! Not even the Christians, God's very own ambassadors on Earth. We were told that not only did the Christians do nothing, many Christian leaders, theologians, and teachers even sided with the Nazis. The anti-semitic support helped contribute to the attempted genocide of the Jews.

The Christians and the Christian leaders? I was appalled. I spent the entire time walking through the museum angry that humanity, in particular my Christians brothers and sisters, would allow this sort of thing to happen. How could they sit in comfort while this mass persecution and execution was happening? After reading and listening to the compelling, heartbreaking stories one after another, I walked out of the museum at a loss for words.

For those who know me, something really big must have been going on if I was at a loss for words. The only other time in my life that I can remember being without words was the time I was playing Scrabble and got stuck with a "g,v,c,z,q," and two "a"'s. How do you do anything in Scrabble with a "q" if you do not have a "u"? Every "q" needs a "u."

It was during this rare speechless moment that God started to press a little harder on my heart. It is easy to blame others, but what would I have done living in Nazi Germany? I, Jon Morrison, a non-Jew, would have been safe from Hitler and the S.S. I got honest that day sitting on a bench outside the Museum thinking that my response would have probably gone something like,

"Man, what's happening to those people is terrible.

Someone should do something to stop it.

I hope someone is doing something to stop it.

I'm sure *someone* is doing something to stop it.

Yes, someone has got to be doing something to stop it.

I should make a sandwich for lunch today."

That was a humbling moment. I realized that there were horrible injustices going on all over the world where people, who bear God's image, were being dehumanized, marginalized, oppressed, ignored, and murdered and I was doing nothing about it.

Darfur. Rwanda. The homeless of the Downtown Eastside in Vancouver. The cries of the poor were being ignored

By me.

I was no better than those Christians who let the Nazis get away with the Holocaust. I was the priest and Levite who walked by the beat up man on the road to Jericho. I was ignoring the other 2100 verses in Scripture where God calls his people to action on social justice issues. Like the part in Isaiah 58 where God tells the Israelites that the reason He is ignoring all their religious worship activities is because they are ignoring the needs of the hungry, oppressed, naked and homeless.

> "Is this not the kind of fasting I have chosen: to loosen the chords of injustice and untie the cords of the yoke, to set the oppressed free and break every yoke? Is it not to share your food with the hungry and to provide the poor wanderer with shelter — when you see the naked to clothe him and not to turn away from your own flesh and blood?[83]"

God's plan for his people was to be concerned about these things and I was not doing that. Not doing what God says to do is called sin. I was sinning and I had to do some repenting right there in Jerusalem that day. It was a defining moment — a moment you have when you know that you are, from that point on, forever changed.

"A broken and contrite heart, O God, you will not despise[84]." C.S. Lewis' definition for a contrite heart is a "crushed and pulverized heart[85]." That is a lot like what I felt. My heart was crushed and pulverized; one, for my selfish hypocrisy, and two, for the hurt and broken of this world who had no one to help them. My heart was finally broken for the things that broke God's heart. I believe God forgave me and was willing to give me another chance.

I made a commitment to Him that day. I told Him I would use whatever influence that He gave me to be a voice for those who had no voice, to fight against injustice around the world, and to defend the rights of the poor and needy however I could. What would that look like back home? The ideas started to flow.

---

[83] Isaiah 58:6-7
[84] Psalm 51:17
[85] Lewis, C.S. *Mere Christianity.* (Harper Books, 1945).

I have always liked to talk; I could use my voice to speak up for those who could not speak for themselves. I was leading a youth group — I could lead my students to the kind of places that Jesus had visited and to hang out with the kind of people that Jesus had hung out with.

This was a hard one. We live in a consumeristic, entertainment based culture and you'd better believe that the "entertain me" attitude of all age groups slips its ugly head into our churches. Hebrews 13:17 talks about how one day leaders will stand before God and be held accountable for how they led God's people. I realized, however, that despite the pressure to entertain teenagers every week, at the end of my life when I stand before God and He asks about my leadership, He is not going to ask why my student's were not better bowlers. He will not hold up a list of other youth group's laser tag scores, and express his disappointment with my underachieving laser snipers.

It is more likely that He's going to ask what we, as His people, did for Jesus when he was around us in the form of the hungry, thirsty, lonely, sick, naked and imprisoned. Jesus said that whenever we take care of those whom our society would deem "least" we are not just taking care of them, but Jesus Himself. In Matthew 25 when Jesus teaches this, He warns that there are eternal consequences to ignoring him in the hungry, thirsty, lonely, sick, naked and imprisoned form.

A Lesson From The King

Psalm 72 is a prayer of a famous King named Solomon who asked God for great riches and influence among all the greatest world leaders. Usually I would not suggest praying along these lines unless, of course, you have Solomon's motives. We see in verses 12 and 13 that the king seeks treasure and influence so he can "deliver the needy who cry out, the afflicted who have no one to help... to take pity on the weak and the needy and save the needy from death[86]."

I understand this kind of prayer because I understand the need for men and women to become champions for those who need champions. So I pray too that God would use me, as well as many wealthy and influential young men and women, to accomplish His purposes for the poor, needy and outcast in our society. My hope is that your young life will be an answer to this prayer.

You may not feel rich and influential, but you are. By being born and educated in the time and location that you currently live in, you have a tremendous amount of potential to do good for the sake of those who do not have the same privilege. What will it take for you to have a defining moment when you realize that God is calling all of us to spend ourselves on behalf of the hungry[87]?

A Need In My Backyard

The Downtown Eastside is an ugly place these days. It is currently the poorest postal code in Canada and has even been declared a state of emergency by the United Nations. Vancouver has a complex homeless problem. I was recently in London, England and met a guy who had heard on the news about Vancouver's rapidly growing number of drug addicted and mentally ill homeless men and women. This internationally notorious problem was going on 20 minutes down the highway from my church, and we were doing nothing about it.

I had to do something. I made a commitment in Jerusalem that I would follow through on my conviction, but was unsure where to start.

---

[86] Psalm 72:12-13
[87] Isaiah 58:10

Putting An Army Together

It was not enough to try to change the world on my own. I was not Spiderman, Superman or Optimis Prime; I was just Jon and, if I'm honest, that isn't very much. God brought some fired up young adults into my life who would become my revolutionary friends. We shared a common passion to reach the Downtown Eastside with the light of Jesus. It is great to look back and observe how God not only provided the conviction to create change, but then also provided the companions to drive the conviction.

I am uneasy making the comparison about what was going on in our lives to a real revolution where governments are overthrown, thousands of people are influenced (or killed), and history is changed. I'm not talking about anything of that magnitude here. A Russian poet named Boris Pasernak said, "It is not revolutions and upheavals that clear the road to new and better days, but someone's soul inspired and set ablaze." A revolution of this sort is not the kind that makes the news. It is a revolution of the heart, of perspective and of sacrifice in my friends and me.

Stumbling Towards Justice

We had no idea what we were doing but we knew it was all God's idea, and we were confident He was going to show us what to do along the way. One Canada Day we ventured Downtown handing out lit sparklers and, not unlike what happens when you mix polar bears and global warming, it was a suitable icebreaker. After our paltry amount of 30 or so sparklers had burned out, we spent the next couple of hours hanging out with whoever would talk to us. We learned names and listened to people's stories — some were absolutely tragic and some were absolutely hilarious. There was such a hunger for someone to sit and just listen to whatever they had to say. In a small way that night, we learned about the deep need that people have to just be treated like humans.

A few days later it was my birthday. I didn't feel like throwing a typical young adult party at some plastic restaurant where they put a stupid hat on you, and give you a single candled piece of cake while the slightly annoyed and embarrassed staff sing, "Happy Birthday." Does anyone like the song "Happy Birthday" anymore? The song is tired. I think we need a new one.

I wanted to celebrate my birthday with my new friends on the street. A few of the revolutionaries agreed to bake cakes, some bought ice cream and others brought pop. We headed into Pigeon Park, a popular hangout for the Vancouver homeless, to see who wanted to have a party with us. The news reported that a stabbing had happened there the night before but it was no longer a crime scene, it was a party venue. We all got really into it and had 100 or so people in attendance. This party was for anyone who missed theirs during the year. It was *our* party!

Riding the success of the birthday, a few weeks later, we again turned Pigeon Park into an outdoor barbeque. We cooked up burgers on location, handed out water, chips, brought a guitar, and had balloons all over — it was now a summer party! But it was getting expensive and exhausting doing all of these one-off events, and though many liked it, we could not keep showing up in their community uninvited. A long-term plan was desperately needed.

Accidently Finding The Front Door Of Our New Home

One day my tallest revolutionary friend, Mike, was walking the streets of Hastings when he spotted a church service full of homeless folks. Mike had walked into Potters Place Mission, which would soon become our new home. So moved and inspired by what he saw going on there, Mike invited some of us to come check the place out as well.

Potters Place Mission soon became our favorite place to go on Tuesday nights. Each week our job was to bring a worship leader, a preacher, and some hands to help serve food. After the service, we would all hang out with whoever wanted to talk. The people at Potters loved the energy and enthusiasm our crew would bring down, and we loved the chance to build friendships and help whoever we could. More and more youth and young adults started showing up. Giving up a Tuesday night was no chore as many were excited to turn off their TVs, power down their computers and break free from their shackles of suburban slavery if only for just one night a week. In Matthew 10:28, Jesus talks about how we should not fear anything that could harm our physical body but only that which can destroy our souls. Suburban life has a way of destroying the human soul.

My students began to develop genuine friendships with homeless people. It was so cool to witness hearts being broken for those who were so broken in our city. The vision that God had given me at the Holocaust museum was actually happening; He was using my small influence to make a difference on the Downtown Eastside.

Have you noticed that people who come back from short-term missions always conclude that they thought they were going to give, when in reality, they got far more out of it than they gave? Potters is like that too. It's a funny thing — you show up carrying the baggage of a long, busy and tiring day and you always leave feeling alive, refreshed, encouraged and empowered. Some nights it is really tough getting out the door to go there, but I'm always thankful I did once the night is done.

I want to be careful not to paint the Downtown Eastside or homeless people in general with a golden brush of naivety. The place has been called a national disaster and, in such an unsettling area, one is to expect a fair share of troubles and incidents. You get this interesting mix of exceeding joy from seeing God work along with an overwhelming burden in learning just how deep, dark and complex the poverty situation really is in Vancouver. Rather than getting discouraged and overwhelmed by the injustices we saw there, God was teaching us a better way to confront injustice — to dance on it.

It is my pleasure to share a few of our dance moves with you.

1. Dancing With Beauty In The Broken

In working with the homeless, you see beauty and brokenness manifesting themselves simultaneously. Here is an example. Before preaching one night I was enjoying the worship time being led by my uber talented friends, Mike and Brett. Mike was on cello and Brett was leading with his guitar. During the set, a homeless guy walked up to the empty drum kit and decided he wanted to join the band. He knew one beat (I will graciously give him that), but he was not very good and everyone was getting distracted. I kept looking over to see if anyone else was becoming as annoyed as I was. Brett look a little annoyed; Mike looked more annoyed.

But the band played on.

With Brett leading away on guitar and vocals, and Mike making a sweet sound on the cello, the hack drummer sounded awful. As a pastor in Canada, you're not supposed to say that people are awful at things, but I cannot think of a more accurate adjective. "Terrible," "horrendous," or "catastrophic" would have worked as well. I wanted to walk over to the awful drummer and tell him to stop... until I got an epiphany of sorts.

This is not awful — this is church! This is what the church is supposed to be like. It's a bunch of people, from all sorts of life stages and experiences, playing music together. You have the beautiful cello and the hack drummer. It's a professional musician and a busker, a businessman and a beggar, a high school student and an addict. They're all there together. That's the harmonious vision of the church that Jesus died to create.

In my own life there are areas full of God's light and places that are dark. There are places where I am strong and places where I am weak. The church needs to be a place where I can come with both and find acceptance. We should be able to come with our light and darkness, strengths and weaknesses, successes and failures, and join in the worship of a God who accepts us as we are and as we accept others.

I am the hack drummer who makes things awkward, but still has a drum to beat.

So rather than walking over and breaking his sticks, it became great music... though only in a metaphorical sense. The guy really couldn't play at all.

2. The Dance Of Learning To Expect The Unexpected

On another night during the music, a strange, unprecedented scene started to unfold — the kind they do not teach you in Bible school. I was sitting beside a man who pulled some heavy chains out of a backpack, and began to wrap them around his hands and stroked them eerily. He was out of the band's sight but since he was beside me, I sat nervously watching this happen. I didn't know why this guy would need to bring chains into Potters or what the whole wrapping them around his hands episode was all about. Searching for reasons, I played a worst-case scenario in my head; he would run up to my friends on the stage and start attacking them with the chains. Before they were hit, I pictured myself running to the rescue by jumping on his back, and taking him down, thereby saving the day.

I am really brave in my own imagination.

109

The good news is that the worship set ended with no chain attack from my pew neighbour. As I got up to preach I had just one more scary thought, "Oh dear, what if the chain guy was waiting to come after the preacher?" I realized that I was the only one who saw that he had chains around his hands! I was trying to figure out how to make my friends aware of the potential beating.

Without knowledge of proper sign language, all I could do was quickly shift my message to something about how Jesus breaks our chains, and gives us peace with our fellow man. It seemed to sink in for I was not attacked that night.

On another bizarre occasion, I vividly remember our friend Rodney coming forward just before the service, collapsing at the front of the stage and confessing his sins to all who were within earshot. He took out his crack pipe and, very much intoxicated, surrendered his addiction to God praying for forgiveness. I went over to hang out with Rodney, and noticed that he had a good three or so inches of plumber's crack exposed in plain sight for all to see. I began to pray for Rodney and his crack problem. I'm sure God knew what crack problem I was talking about, but an answer to either would have been most appreciated.

I do not understand a lot that goes on at Potters. I still do not know why a guy would bring chains to church or why Rodney did not have a belt on. But Potters is an honest place because my friends there cannot pretend to have it all together like we do in the suburbs. Homeless folks wear their brokenness on their sleeves while we try to hide ours. They do not have anything with which to make masks while we spend our whole lives constructing images of someone we're not. When homeless people feel deep pain and despair, many of them cope with drugs and alcohol. When suburban people feel deep pain and despair, many of them use prescription drugs which often leads to copious amounts of Ikea.

It's all the same, just a bit different. Sometimes I wonder who is more sick, us or them.

I starting coming to Potters to help lead people out of their brokenness, but the truth is that they are leading me out of mine. In their honesty I learn to be honest. In their pain I learn to face my own pain. With their perspective I learn perspective.

3. Dancing With Creativity

New creative ideas about how to fight poverty began to rise to the surface. One of my grade twelve students, Cam, needed to do a work experience project for graduation and I challenged him to pursue his real passions rather than just following a typical work experience route. While most kids were doing internships through trades or local firms, Cam wanted to run a citywide campaign to raise money and fight homelessness in our city. In need of help to pull the idea off, we grabbed a couple of Cam's friends and formed a team in hopes that God would use the idea to make a real difference in the city.

We called it the *Dollar A Day Campaign*. By taking on something that was "city wide," we needed every opportunity to spread the vision of Dollar A Day. No one had ever tried anything like this, so it was a lot of work trying to find opportunities to promote the cause. We needed some help from Jesus to pull it off.

I love the story found in all four gospels of Jesus feeding five thousand people with a kid's fish and bread. It reminds me a lot of my Dollar A Day experience. In the story, the disciples come up to Jesus with a problem. "Lord, these people have been hanging around with us all day. They are hungry." Jesus' solution to the disciples is simple but a little unrealistic. "Ok, you feed them." The disciples respond quite pragmatically, "We do not have enough food to give or money to foot the bill for a caterer." Jesus responds, "What do you have? Give it to me." The disciples collect a few loaves and fish, and present it to the one who would soon be remembered for executing the greatest feeding miracle in history. He takes the disciple's offering, blesses it, and feeds the people.

That's a bit what it was like trying to run Dollar A Day in our first year. Like the disciples, our Dollar A Day crew came to Jesus and said, "Hey Jesus, these people are homeless, they need your help." We told Jesus about the homeless problem and He told us to do something about it. We said we couldn't due on our own personal limitations. He said the same thing to us as He had to the disciples some two thousand years ago,

"Give it to me."

So we gave him the best we had, and watched him pull off a few miracles.

One of those miracles came on a particular Tuesday night at Potters. In passing I was told by one of the guys about a citywide event about two months away at GM Place Stadium (where the Canucks play) for Canada Day. It was to be the one year anniversary of our initial sparkler party Downtown. Knowing that this would be a good opportunity to promote the campaign, I called up the organizer of the event and asked if we could have some time to do an announcement for Dollar A Day during the rally. It was a bit of a long shot but,

She said yes.

What? We were really allowed to do an announcement? I couldn't believe it. There was only one announcement that night and Dollar A Day did it! God had opened a door and we decided to make the most of it. On Canada Day, Cam, Mike and I stood holding lit sparklers in front of 11,000 fired up Christians announcing this campaign run by a grade 12 student and his sidekick, the youth pastor.

Remember what I said before about stepping out? You just put yourself out there and do it.

Our plan was to get as many people as possible from the event to walk down to Hastings Street, light up the 7,500 sparklers that we had bought, and celebrate Canada Day right there on our favourite corner of the city, Pigeon Park.

Outside of Potters Place Mission we had a full band set up. We sang "Oh Canada," "Amazing Grace," and proceeded to worship in the streets for the next hour or two. Those who could stop to count that night estimated the number to be around 800 worshippers on Hastings Street. We shut down two, sometimes three, lanes of traffic as we danced and sang with our lit sparklers.

It was a night to remember — a preview of what heaven will be like. The rich and the poor from many cultures coming together to celebrate Jesus, the one who came to bring "good news to the poor, to bind up the brokenhearted, to proclaim freedom for the captives, and to release them from the darkness[88]."

Dollar A Day enjoyed great favour earning local and national media coverage. In the first year, I was very proud of my revolutionary students who put on fundraisers, all nighters, and went door-to-door collecting money from friends, family and neighbors. It was exciting to see high school students championing all the causes that God had convicted me so heavily on just one year prior. We started to "get it," and the excitement that came with the process was great.

I Need The Poor

You might read a chapter like this and feel guilted into helping the homeless or to take on a social justice issue around the

---

[88] Luke 4:18–19

world. You may be watching TV and see a news report and think,

"I should really do something."

So you take a night to hand out socks or give a dollar to a guy you pass by on the street and, even though you're certain it will not accomplish what you are hoping it to do, it eases your conscience just a bit — at least for awhile.

Guilt is a bad reason to do anything in life. To experience authentic passion, excitement, adventure, risk, struggle, joy, satisfaction, encouragement, and purpose are all great reasons to do anything! I've found all of the above to be true since God called me to get out of my comfort based lifestyle and get involved in social justice issues around the world. The need has never been greater, except the need is more in me than anywhere else.

Something happens inside of you when you serve a meal to someone that has not eaten in days. There is a God-given joy in giving a blanket to someone you know would have frozen without it or in sharing the hope of Jesus to a man who has confessed he is about to give up on life. The adrenaline, the rush, the exhaustion at the end of the day knowing you have given a human being hope to live on — we need to feel it. It does something in your soul that cannot necessarily be articulated, just felt.

I suppose Oscar Schindler and the other 13,999 Europeans who risked their lives to save the Jewish people would agree with me.

I am so grateful for God's gift to me that day at the Holocaust Museum. I would hope that you experience the blessing of having your heart crushed and pulverized as well one day. When it first happened, I thought God was calling me to change some things around the world. Now I realize that the most change God wanted to do was inside of me. Those I thought I was helping were, in reality, helping me.

Those are just a few of my stories about how God made me comfortable about getting *un*comfortable for the rest of my life.

Now go and ask Jesus to help you write your own, and may it be the kind of story that is worth telling.

Of Friends And Noses.

Pick one or both but not at the same time

"Do not be misled: Bad company corrupts good character."
1 Corinthians 15:33

Sure, it has been ten years but I can still remember a few things from high school. I remember how important it was to have people around you called "friends." In high school, I was certainly not the most popular, but I was not the least popular either. I had found a comfortable middle rung on the popularity ladder with my jock buddies. I was okay with this position because we had each other. We were brothers, and in it for the long haul no matter what was going to come our way. My grade twelve yearbook is full of promises suggesting this sort of eternal brotherhood. Here are a couple of things my "friends for life" wrote:

"Dude, we are going to be friends for life!"

"This summer is going to be awesome. We are going to hang out all the time!"

"You are like a brother to me!"

Then all of a sudden, we closed our yearbooks and graduated. Since that day, I have seldom seen any of these "eternal brothers". It's sad but it happens all the time to people graduating from high school.

It was the friends I made in the years following my high school graduation that have helped me become the person that I am today, and I am more convinced that they will be in my life forever. This chapter is about looking at the friends in your life and deciding if you want these people to determine your destiny as a human being.

Dragging You Down Or Saving Your Life?

One spring I was feeling a little bored with life, so I decided to cross a few of the things off of the "Things I Want To Do Before I Die" list. I had tried bungee jumping, so I naturally decided to progress to the next thing on my list, skydiving. I was given a tight bright purple jumpsuit that made me look like Tinky Winky from Teletubbies. I could have felt emasculated in that bright purple suit, but I didn't allow that to affect me — I was going to jump out of a plane and that was tough enough for me!

After spending a short amount of time in training, I made the walk to the plane and was surprised to find that it was very small. Maybe it was the size of the plane or perhaps the sound of the propellers whirring around and around, but at that moment I felt my nerves kick in. I quickly hopped in and it soon became apparent that any apprehensions I might have with this mission were soon going to be too late.

BAM! The door closed and we took off. I watched the height climb from 1000 feet to 3000 feet and keep climbing until we finally reached 12,000 feet. From that height, it is amazing to see everything on such a small scale and I will admit that I enjoyed the opportunity to take it all in. However, my euphoric moment came to an abrupt halt when the door slid open, and I remembered why I was flying in the first place.

My guide looked at me and said, "Okay, out you go."

Instantly, it was gut check time. I was about to jump out of a plane. I had talked about it, blogged about it, paid for it, written my will, put on a sissy little purple jump suit, and gotten into the plane — now it was time to actually make the jump.

Gulp. As I write this, my stomach is reminding me just what it was like. Nausea. Legs feeling like jelly. Nervousness. Fear. Adrenaline... and then I was jumping and falling!

The rush of free falling was unlike anything I had ever felt before. Almost immediately, I realized that I was taking a direct route straight to the ground by virtue of falling extremely fast from an extreme height. Until that point, my thoughts had been focused on getting out of the plane. I had never thought much about whether or not the parachute was packed right or what that whole experience would be like. What if...? Nah. I continued hurtling towards the earth. The wind was howling past my ears and the ground was getting closer and closer with every passing second. After screaming a little on the outside to match the screaming going on inside of me, I looked over my shoulder and there was my assurance that this skydiving adventure was not going to be a fatal endeavor. I found my hope in the form of...

A man strapped to my back? Yes, a man strapped to my back!

In the skydiving world, it would be silly if, on your first jump, they threw you out a plane to fend for yourself. Instead, everyone is required to take a few jumps with an instructor. I had a guy attached to my back the whole time who thankfully was an expert at skydiving, parachute packing and at knowing exactly when it was time to end our free fall and release the parachute. Because of him, I thankfully landed safely on the ground alive and well.

So what does this story mean to you? I think there are two ways that you can apply this story to your life. Let's take a "choose your own application" approach when it comes to the friendships in your life.

Option One: You and your friends are jumping out of planes together attached at the hip. Each one of you is making bad choices in your life. Sticking with my story, when one friend makes a bad choice, it drags both the decision-maker and the other friend to the ground at a much faster rate. To make matters worse, each of you is completely unaware that the decisions you are making are leading to dangerous consequences that will inevitably end in a deadly collision with the ground. You each assume the other is in full control of the situation. You and your friend are both trusting that the other knows how to pack a parachute and pull the release cord when, in truth, both of you forgot the backpack in the plane.

Option Two: You and your friends are jumping out of planes together and you are attached at the hip. In this scenario, you have predetermined who is going to be the one responsible for packing the parachute and pulling the cord. Together, you enjoy a "pleasant" jump creating a lifelong experience that will be a fond memory for the rest of your lives. You are able to work together and support each other through the experience.

So which application best describes the experience of you and your friends?

A Proverb Worth Living

The book of Proverbs is a book about wisdom. For the purpose of our discussion, wisdom is defined as knowing what is right and wrong and then choosing to do the right thing. The "wise-guy" writer of Proverbs was a man named Solomon, who also just happened to be the King of Israel. He wrote about the importance of choosing your close friends wisely because those you hang out with or call friend will determine the quality and direction of your life. Proverbs 13:20 says, "He who walks with the wise grows wise, but a companion of fools suffers harm."

If you value being wise, that is, if you value not destroying your life like a train wreck and causing all those around you to suffer for your foolish choices, you would do well to apply this proverb to your life. If you do, the promise is that you will yourself become wise. Should you fail to heed God's teaching, the end of the verse explicitly warns about your inevitable suffering.

Let me say one thing about gaining wisdom. I have found that there are two ways to gain wisdom. One way is to listen to the wisdom in the form of advice, counsel, or proverb, trust it and then do what it says. For example, common wisdom states that it is foolish to send a text message while driving, as it will inevitably result in a car accident. Choosing not to send text messages while driving is wisdom in action. The second way to gain wisdom is the hard way and is often referred to as learning a lesson. This method often involves gaining wisdom shortly after you needed it. Of course, this is a much more expensive, time consuming, emotionally taxing, physically draining and spiritually costly way to learn, but it is a time-honoured teacher for many of us.

How Much Influence Do They Have?

Take a moment to do this quick test to see just how influential your friends are in shaping who you are:

1. Have you ever made a decision that went against your own personal beliefs and values because your friends placed pressured on you to do so?

2. Have you ever compromised something that you knew God didn't want you to do but, because your friends were doing it, you decided to go along with them?

3. Have you ever really wanted to do something or go somewhere but chose not to because your friends wanted to do something else?

If you answered yes to any of the above three questions then you, like most of us, are highly influenced by your friends. You need to start taking Proverbs 13:20 seriously.

Next time you are hanging out with your friends, I recommend taking a good long look (maybe not too directly because that's awkward) at the people you call friends. Then start by asking yourself, "Do I want to become just like these people? Do I like who they are? Do I like where they are headed?"

It is good to ask yourself these hard questions, because the answers you formulate will allow you to determine how your friends are influencing you. As sure as the sun will rise tomorrow, the more time you hang out with your friends, the more you will start to look, sound, and behave like them. You will dress like them and talk like them. You will read the books they read and watch the movies they watch. If they get tattoos, you will probably get tattoos as well. If they get piercings, it is likely that you too will get piercings in the same places. Most importantly, you and your friends will, at the very least, begin to share the same values, which means that you will all be heading in the same direction.

For many people, sharing values, doing similar things, and traveling through life together is a good thing.

We Need Each Other

Your friends can be one of your greatest strengths. They can make you a better person. In Ephesians 6, Paul tells the people at the church of Ephesus to approach life as a spiritual battle, and to be armed with the full armour of God: the helmet, breastplate, belt, shield, shoes, and sword. In the original Greek translation, the imperative of "put on" is written in the second person plural, which indicates it is a command not to individuals, but to two or more people. By knowing this fact, it is not such a stretch to suggest that Paul was instructing the entire community to arm themselves for battle together. Personally, I need a community of friends to help me in a battle because, left alone, I can be horrendously unprepared for the challenges of war. The truth is that I can't find my sword, I forget my helmet at home, and I may want to settle for a lazy nap underneath a shady tree instead of fighting. With friends fighting beside me, my life is different. A friend can be there to roust you out of bed and get you excited for battle while handing you a sword and lending you their shield. This is why we need each other.

On the other hand, a friend could tell you that shields, swords, and helmets are items found in fairy tales and then pass you some cocaine.

Who would I rather be friends with? Hmmm, I'm no rocket surgeon but I will take the first group and keep my criminal record clear for the time being.

Your friends determine the quality and direction of your life. Period.

This is one area in my life where I have full confidence in saying that God has been exceedingly gracious, and that I have made wise decisions when it has come to choosing friends. If there is anything about me that is honourable and worthwhile, then it is my testimony about the faithfulness of God and the goodness of the people with whom God has surrounded me. I have become a product of the people that I choose to spend my time with. Their character traits started to become my traits. Take my tall friend Mike for instance; he is a passionate revolutionary and can convince me that a couple of single guys in their mid-twenties really can change the world. I never fully believe him, but at least we get really excited when discussing the possibilities over a good coffee. When I want to wrestle with some deep and seemingly unsolvable theological issues, I hang out with my Scottish friend Dave, the Calvinist. He is one of the smartest guys I know though he is 5 years my junior. When I need wisdom, insight and perspective, I call up one of my two "wise guy" friends, both named Jeremy. Two of my favourite people in the world are Stu and Tim. I love them even though they live in Calgary. These are my boys who I can instantly laugh with and, at the same time, we challenge each other to become stronger and more faithful men of God.

That is how my friends influence me. How about yours? Who are the people you go to?

You Choose

Friendships do not often "just happen;" you have to choose them. This means that *not* choosing your friends wisely is still a choice. How do you make good c4hoices when it comes to making friends? I would suggest starting with a look inside yourself; find out what you value, what your goals are, who do you want to become, and then find people who share those things. For example:

Do you want to do well in university? Hang around people who have the same dreams. They will influence the way you pay attention in class, and whether you choose to study hard or party hard the night before a midterm.

Do you want to be able to hold down a good job? Become friends with people who are hard working, who don't value spending an entire week playing video games and who see the light of day before noon.

Do you want to be a happier and more pleasant person? Make a point to seek out people who are happy, pleasant people and spend time with them. Their positive outlook on life will rub off on you and your pessimistic, critical spirit will hopefully fade.

Do you want to grow in your love for God and relationship with Jesus? Hang out with people who share your faith and do not take joy in seeing you shipwreck yourself on the rocks and crags of other worldviews.

By words and actions you will "spur one another on towards love and good deeds[89]."

So what about being friends with people that aren't Christians? Well, in my opinion I don't think that it is smart to only have Christian friends. You are going to encounter all sorts of interesting people during your lives. In fact, I am certain that you have probably met some of them already. Take time to understand them and love them because this is what Jesus commanded us to do in the Great Commission. But also remember that these people do not share the same foundational belief system that you have. Because of this fact, there will be major differences in the way they rationalize their decisions and behaviours. So know what you believe and make sure they know it too. If they are truly your friends, they will respect you and seek to understand you. I will leave you with one piece of advice on this topic. When you step out into the world with your non-believing friends, make sure you are the one doing the influencing — hopefully this will mean that during a party you will not be the one passed out on the floor with a lampshade on your head. That is definitely not the kind of influence you want to have.

Every Paul Needs A Barnabas

In Acts 9, we are first introduced to the Apostle Paul. It was this man who would become the most successful church planter in

---

[89] Hebrews 10:24

the history of the world and would write a majority of the New Testament. Before becoming Christianity's poster boy, we first meet Paul as a critically judgmental man who was spending his time as the deadly persecutor of the Christians. He hated anyone who followed Jesus and wanted nothing more than to see them dead. However, Paul soon converted to Christianity when the risen Jesus appeared to him on a road and told him to stop being such an idiot. Having met Jesus personally, Paul was radically transformed and zealously started preaching about his new faith in Jesus to anyone who would listen. He tried to arrange a meeting with the church leaders, who were the original disciples of Jesus, but they had only heard of Paul's past life and were too scared to give him a chance in person. Personally, I don't blame them. But things had changed. Paul was a new man and needed a second chance; he needed someone who would believe in him and teach him a few things about life as a follower of Jesus. He needed a friend.

Along came a man named Barnabas whose name means, "son of encouragement." How about that for a name? If I had a friend named "Encouragement," I would probably never leave that friend's side. We would always get invited to parties and probably get a lot of free coffees at Starbucks just because that friend would be so darn encouraging. As it turns out, Barnabas' character was as true as his name suggests. Eugene Peterson's *The Message* translates Acts 9:26 as, "Barnabas took Paul under his wing[90]." I love that. Barnabas or "Encouragement," as we could call him, saw a young man that was rough around the edges but full of exciting potential. Barnabas showed Paul around, taught him about Jesus, introduced him to a few people, and probably helped him plan for his future ministry.

Barnabas had a profound impact on Paul's life and the two became great friends by going on church planting road trips together. Paul is hailed as the greatest missionary in Christian history. The spread of Christianity through Asia Minor, the

---

[90]   Peterson, Eugene. *The Message.* (Navpress, 2000)

Roman Empire and subsequently Europe and even North America can be traced back to Paul's work. I'm sure if Paul were able to speak to us today, he would tell us with tremendous gratitude about his encouraging friend Barnabas. He would tell us how Barnabas was willing to be his friend by nurturing his potential and "take him under his wing."

I know what it is like to need a wing to take shelter under. Going through my teenage years was an awkward ordeal. I was introduced to girls, zits, high school, sports, climbing and sliding on the popularity ladder, youth group, puberty, God, doubts, plus a load of crazy and mysterious questions. I definitely had a whole bunch of new experiences to process, which would have been really difficult to do alone. I thank God for the Spirit-filled men that He put in my life like my dad, my friends Clint, Grant, Craig, Dave and Bill. Those guys took an interest in my life deciding that my well being and sanity was worth their time. They believed that I was worth it and invested themselves in me for the purpose of seeing that I made it through school alive.

These mentors of mine took time to be with me and to listen to my stories. They would offer guidance and wisdom, which has helped me develop into a man, leader and a follower of Jesus. These memories are what I remember best about growing up with older men in my life. It was great hanging out in the fun, euphoric times, but it was especially great to have someone older with perspective when it felt like my dramatic teenage life was falling apart. They were there after all the breakups, the stupid mistakes, the bad hockey games and the times when I was on the brink of giving up on Christianity altogether.

I do not remember much about what I learned in youth group or recall many of the sermons I sat through, but I do remember these men vividly and I am eternally grateful for the impact that they had on my life. Simply said, I am who I am today because of those guys. In addition to those guys, I continue to seek out older, wiser men that will speak into my life because I believe that a mentor is an invaluable friend that everyone should have.

By working in youth ministry, I am confronted daily with the fact that it is important to have people in your life who are a little further along life's road and are completely committed to telling you about their experiences. The people that make up the Coquitlam Alliance youth staff are my heroes. They are part superhero, part counselor, part chauffeur, part cheerleader, part coach, part teammate, part disciplinarian, part shoulder to cry on, part pastor and part teacher. The simple fact is that they do it all!

If you do not have a person like this in your life, then you need to find one. You need a mentor because life can be difficult and deceiving if left on your own. That being the case, a person that can listen to your experiences and offer Godly counsel, as well as tell you about their own experiences, is awesome. Trust me, no one has enough life experience to go it alone. Your friends are neither wise enough nor smart enough to fill this role for you. So how do you find a mentor? It is actually quite simple:

First and foremost, you need to pray. Ask God to show you the right person to approach. Secondly, trusting that God is at work in your life, think about the people around you that you want to be like. It could be anyone that you feel has characteristics that you would like to have passed on to you. Once you have done this, you need to complete the following steps:

1. Contact them. This can be in person, by phone, email or whatever.
2. Ask them. "Could you be my mentor?" works well. "Can we hang out?" will also work and is a little less formal.
3. Wait for their response.

If they say, "Yes," then congratulations, you have found yourself a mentor. If they decline for whatever reason, repeat steps 1–4 until you get an affirmative response from someone and do not give up!

Every Paul Needs A Timothy

Jesus recruited a lunch pail crew of young men to be his disciples. These guys were to be the ones who would closely follow him for three years, and then spread the message about the kingdom of God on earth. In Matthew 10:8, Jesus sends out his newly recruited disciples on a short term mission trip and gives them a command to live by on their trip. I have taken this command seriously and I hope you will too. So what is it? Stop consuming and start serving others, "freely you have received, now freely give."

I like using this verse at grad nights because if you have been raised in the church, you most likely have been taking a lot without giving enough. Why do I say this? Well, if you grew up in church, you went through some form of Sunday school and then, whether forced by your parents or voluntarily, you moved on to some form of youth group, which you attended until graduation. During this time you had teachers, mentors, and pastors who loved you and decided to pour their time, energy and money into your life. If you are like I was when I attended youth, your youth leaders will be able to point to several grey hairs that they have named after you and your "Reign of Terror" in the youth group.

Have you heard it said, "It takes a whole village to raise a child?" Well if you haven't, then get out of that rock you've been hiding under and let me tell you it's a true statement. In addition to your parents, there have been teachers, coaches, extended family, friends, friend's parents and community leaders. All of these people have invested a great deal of themselves into you to see that you made it thus far. They wanted you to graduate alive, while being ready to take on life's challenges. A great deal of prayer, energy, sweat and even some blood went into preparing you for success. Freely you have received.

Now, it is time for you to freely give. It is time to start pouring yourself into someone else. Someone needs to be taught the lessons that you have learned; someone needs to be warned not to walk down roads that you should have never walked down. Someone needs to talk through their problems with an older friend that they can trust. Someone needs you.

Imagine who you would be if you'd had no help getting to where you are today. What if there is a person out there today, much like you were when you were a young teenager, who needs you around in their life? Okay, I can hear some you saying to me through the page, I did not have anyone there in those darkest moments, so what's the big deal? How comforting would it have been to have had someone to help you sort through your emotions, problems or just to make you laugh? How great would it have been to have had someone to let you know they loved you and were praying for you? You can be that someone that you never had.

The Apostle Paul had a great deal of help from Barnabas but he also devoted himself to helping a young leader named Timothy. Paul took Timothy under his own proverbial wing. In fact, Paul wrote two letters to his young protégé that were so influential that they were passed around churches, preserved and now exist today in our Bibles as First and Second Timothy. They are two of my favourite books in the Bible because they give us an inside look at how Paul mentored Timothy. So, let's take a look at the wisdom Paul passed on.

1. Being An Authentic Example

"Here is a trustworthy saying that deserves full acceptance: Christ Jesus came into the world to save sinners — of whom I am the worst. But for that very reason I was shown mercy so that in me, the worst of sinners, Christ Jesus might display his unlimited patience as an example for those who would believe on him and receive eternal life.[91]"

Paul gave Timothy a backstage pass into his own life. He allowed Timothy to see his struggles and hear the story of God's grace in his life, which gave Timothy insight into the very heart of his mission. Paul was living with Jesus in every facet of his life and this was an example to Timothy in the truest sense. French philosopher Albert Sweitzer once noted that when wanting to successfully influence others, the example you set before them is not the main thing; it's the only thing of importance. A good mentor will live his or her life with integrity and will model good character. The result is that it will be transferred like static electricity to those that are looking to that person for mentorship.

2. Strength and Encouragement

> "Don't let anyone look down on you because you are young, but set an example for the believers in speech, in life, in love, in faith and in purity[92]."

Paul believed that his young friend was a very capable leader right away. He wanted to make sure that Timothy did not get discouraged by those who would suggest he was too young to be used by God. I would imagine that those would have been timely words for the young and impressionable Timothy to hear as his older critics might have intimidated him.

3. Challenging

> "Watch your life and doctrine closely. Persevere in them, because if you do, you will save both yourself and your hearers[93]."

---

[91] 1 Timothy 1:1-16
[92] 1 Timothy 4:12
[93] 1 Timothy 4:16

Paul was not afraid to give Timothy strict commands. In order to be an effective leader, Paul knew that you must have character *and* sound doctrine. There are many temptations for a young leader, and giving in to them would compromise Timothy's integrity and wipe out his ministry as a leader in the church. "Flee from the evil desires of youth[94]," Paul commands. Many potentially great "would be" leaders abandon their faith by choosing instead to follow the cares of this world. As a result, they end up discounting themselves as leaders of God's people. Timothy would have also been tempted to give in to the culturally popular false teaching that was spreading throughout the church during his time. In response to this, Paul told Timothy, hold on to what I taught you, what Jesus taught us and do not teach anything else.

Mentoring Is Good For You Too

The benefit of pouring your life into another person is worth mentioning too. I know it sounds selfish to say that you will gain something from giving yourself to others, but I think God made us that way. There is a deep sense of satisfaction that comes from helping another human being through the gift of sharing. You could share your experience, your time or your patience but no matter what it is, you are making a big difference in the life of someone that needs you.

I have benefited a great deal from the time I have spent with my friend Cam. Though he is almost ten years my junior, he is an amazing friend who has taught me a great deal. His passion and enthusiasm for the causes of Christ leave me challenged every time we meet. While I like to think of myself as one of Cam's mentors, I often think that he has poured more into my life than he even realizes. I believe this is one of God's greatest gifts to a mentor. I hope you can share in it as well.

---

[94] 2 Timothy 2:22

Cam also keeps me humble. One night while I was preaching at youth, Cam was upstairs in the sound booth dozing off. My sermon was interrupted by a loud crash that startled everyone in attendance that night. Unsure of what happened, we all feared the worst for Cam's safety as he was the only person in the balcony that night. I lost sympathy for him when I learned the true story for the source of the crash. Cam was bored with my sermon, fell asleep and tumbled off his chair. It was humbling to me and Cam learned his lesson to pay attention when the Word of God is being preached.

Be A Hero

I had a defining moment come one afternoon while watching the epic superhero sequel, *Spiderman 2*[95]. It came in the scene just after Peter Parker gives up his superhero alter ego as Spiderman to pursue a normal life away from fighting crime. Of course, there is a girl on the line and rightly so, he wants to get to know her without Spiderman getting in the way. Peter's move was understandable. Mary Jane is the type of girl that you want to give up the red and black jammies for. But then something happens that Peter didn't see coming. Peter runs into a downtrodden neighbourhood kid dragging his feet around because Spiderman is out of the life-saving/crime-solving business. When Peter digs a bit deeper, he gets an explanation from Aunt May about why the kid is so bummed out. The kid had lost his hero. May explains it to Peter this way.

> "Everybody needs a hero, courageous sacrificing people, setting examples for all of us. Everybody loves a hero, people line up for them, cheer for them, scream their names, and years later tell how they stood in the rain for hours just to get a glimpse of the one who told them to hold on a second longer. I believe there's a hero in all of us, that keeps us honest, gives us strength, makes us

[95]

noble. And finally gets us to die with pride. Even though sometimes we have to be steady and give up the thing we want most, even our dreams."

Who is going to wait in the rain for you? Whose hope are you restoring with your encouragement to hold on "just a second longer?" Who will you be a hero to?

Give yourself away to someone. Become a hero to a kid by volunteering to be a youth leader at church, a coach to a team or a volunteer at a summer camp.

Freely you have received, now freely give. These friendships will affect the direction and quality of your life.

A Few More Notes On Friendships

There are just a few more things that I want to say about friendships that did not really fit the above paragraphs but I feel are still worth mentioning. I'm a little ashamed that I feel I have to include some of these.

Hanging out online is not hanging out

We live in a world where communication between friends has never been easier. Social networking through online communities is an effective way to contact your friends. It is a means to an end though. Chatting online, writing notes, emails, text messages, etc., are not good ways to keep in touch with people who live 15 minutes from your house. The best way to keep in touch with such friends is to actually hang out with them face to face. Humans were made by God to connect this way. Even the most introverted and the shyest of all the shy people need connections with living people. It gives us life. We were not made to have 15 conversations at once while sitting alone in a dark basement. That's how people go crazy.

Friends come and go; you had best accept it

With online networking so mainstream, it is very easy to keep in touch with friends who live far away from you. Just because communication with long distance friends is available does not necessarily make it mandatory. I'm giving you permission to not feel burdened to keep in touch with everyone. You need to understand that in the coming years you will make many friends. The more places you go and the more experiences you have, the more you will begin to compartmentalize your friendship circles (i.e. These are my high school friends, these are my college friends, these are my friends I met while traveling and these people only think I'm their friend). Because of time constraints, it is impossible to stay as close to all of these people as you once were. You need to give people the grace and the space to drift away from you while not making them feel guilty for making new friends. You should also expect the same grace and space to be given to you as you meet new people. Imagine trying to keep in touch with everyone all the time. You would do nothing but talk on the phone and email, and we've already mentioned that this sort of basement dwelling is to be avoided.

Be a friend to make a friend

Robert Putnam recently wrote a book called *Bowling Alone*[96]. He observed that Americans (and Canadians too) are becoming increasingly disconnected from each other in our families, neighbourhoods, churches, schools, etc. The statistics show that we, as a society, are getting lonelier and lonelier. We belong to fewer organizations and clubs, know our neighbours less, and hang out with our friends and families less often. As Putnam's title suggests, we are also bowling alone more often. More Americans are bowling than ever before, but they are not bowling in groups, they are just bowling alone. Who bowls alone? Maybe it is just me but isn't the best part of

---

[96] Putnam, Robert. *Bowling Alone* (Simon and Schuster, 2000).

bowling the round of high-fives you get after bowling a perfect strike? Putnam says the high-five experience is on the decline. He traces how changes in work, family structure, television, computer technology, suburban life, gender roles (i.e. women's roles in society), and other factors have all contributed to this decline and the subsequent loneliness epidemic.

So take a look around — what do you think? Personally, I don't think it takes long to notice that we are a lonely culture. Certainly, there is no doubt about it. Just ask your local pharmacist. Antidepressant use has been on the rise every year since the drugs were introduced.

To be counter cultural in your time, you must declare war on loneliness with every part of your being. God wired you for relationships. He placed a natural need in us for connections with other people. If you do not fill that need with real people rather than just e-people, like Warlocks, Merlins or Guild Leaders, then you will surely spiral into loneliness and depression. Have you noticed that a night at home watching movies or TV just makes you feel emptier than before? What happens when someone does that night after night? The more you hang out alone, the more you only like being by yourself and it gets easier and easier to be away from others. Isolation and bitterness follow shortly after. You have to break the spiral. If you have no one calling you, pick up the phone and make the first call. You have to put yourself out there. Volunteering your time for an organization or cause is a good way to meet people who share the same passions as you. Say "yes" to every invitation to social gatherings even if you feel tired. Stay late but do not be the awkward person who sticks around just a little too long. Take an interest in other people by asking questions and not just talking about yourself. This is annoying. Don't sit around waiting for friends to come to you, go and be a friend to somebody. It's just that simple.

Take the white cords out of your ears for friend's sake!

The more you listen to your iPod, the lonelier you get. That's my theory anyway. This may just be a Jon Morrison soap box moment, but I start twitching when I see two people hanging out together both listening to their iPods. They are together but they are very much isolated. "Easy old man," you may say, "you just don't understand." Oh, I do understand — I understand that it's stupid. There's no connection or conversation, just more isolation. If you're with a friend, turn every device off and talk to each other! This is what normal people do; it's time to get used to it. In addition, you cannot send a text message, email or whatever and hold a real life conversation. So put your iPods and phones down, and go be a friend.

I Kissed Courting Goodbye

And a few other cheeky things to include in a dating chapter.

"You have to kiss a few frogs before you find your Prince Charming."

My aunt and uncle told me at grad that, "The person you marry is the second most important decision you will make in your life so choose wisely." That was great advice and it is the best thing you can take from this chapter.

The rest is just my opinion. According to Alex Hitchens, the main character in the movie *Hitch*, you can have success in your relationships if you stick to this one basic principle: there are no basic principles. I would never write a "Seven Easy Steps To Make Sure She Says 'Yes'", or "How To Find The Perfect Guy" kind of chapter because there are no seven easy steps for you and there are certainly no perfect guys out there. I only have a little bit of wisdom that I have learned over the years to humbly offer you. Keep what you like and throw away the rest. If it is true that "wisdom is what you gain just after you really need it,"

Then I have a lot of wisdom.

The Dating Game

Dating may not be the best system out there, but my guess is that it will be the one you choose when it comes to finding the right mate for you. One thing that I have observed about the dating process is the high amount of emotional turmoil it generates for all those involved in it. You have to go through a lot if you want to be a participant in the dating game. This has been my experience with the taxing process of trying to start a relationship. Girls, I'm sure there is a whole other side, but this is the struggle from a guy's perspective, at least the one I can attest to.

Step One: Break The Ice

You spot them across the room, at church, in a coffee shop, wherever. They are the perfect match for you! Now all you must do is find out who they are. Making the initial contact with a stranger you are attracted to is half the battle and an extremely difficult part of said battle. When is the right time to make your approach? What should you say to this person? What if you say something stupid? What if they're already in a relationship? What if you get shot down, crash and hit the ground right there in front of everyone? It's tough stuff to make that initial contact.

Here are five conversation starters that I promise will never work:

5. "My buddies and I have a bet going, you're a girl right?"
4. "I am very lonely person... My mom said I should get off the computer and..."
3. "I'm starting a petition to get George Bush elected as Prime Minister of Canada, would you like to sign?"
2. "Have you heard that Jon Morrison wrote a book?"
1. "Baby, my love for you is like diarrhea, I just can't hold it in any longer!"

As difficult as it is to make the right first impression, the stats would suggest that a simple, "Hello" has a tremendous success rate when it comes to breaking the ice.

Step Two: Making The Call

Let's say you manage to make contact — things go well and you exchange numbers. Now it opens up a whole new bunch of questions. When do you call? The next day shows that you are interested but a little needy. Waiting another day shows that you are not desperate but who has the patience to wait that long? Maybe you could send a harmless text first? But how many texts per day is too many? What happens if you call them and they do not pick up? Do you leave a message or try again later? Should you sound funny or clever or stick to business, "Hi, it's me. Call me back. Bye."

Step Three: The First Date

Once phone contact has been made, a first date is then arranged. This is the start of the lengthy interview process to fill the vacant position of "Lifetime Mate."

A guy has to go through a debate inside his head before suggesting the proper first date location: Do you keep it simple, stick with the safe route and "go for coffee?" Do you eat a meal and pray that nothing gets stuck in your teeth, spilled on your shirt or answered with your mouth full of food? Do you go all out planning an elaborate evening that's full of surprises and flare from start to finish? Girls want the guy to at least *seem* like he has a plan, but the wrong plan could be disastrous for the budding yet very fragile relationship. Choosing the wrong venue like an underground dog fighting tournament would be disastrous while choosing the right place would be... "just perfect."

First dates are tough because both people are brand new to each other. You do not understand each other's jokes,

141

mannerisms, or quirks. You don't know when they're being serious, and half of your best material goes right over their head. A first date is the time to be on your best behaviour, and on constant watch not to do or say anything stupid. Who you are is a fluid concept at this point. You are careful not to be yourself but rather whoever your date wants you to be in order to win at least a second date.

Though you're as fake as a three dollar bill, on a date you're hoping that they're at least being honest enough to give you a good idea of who they really are. You're constantly evaluating things they're doing. It's tough to judge if you want to spend the rest of your life with someone when you do not even know how to properly spell their last name, and just accidently called them the name of your ex-girlfriend.

But dating is an agreed upon interview process, and so the two of you go back and forth asking each other questions that you would never ask a regular human being in any other scenario: "If you could live on a planet and could take only one domesticated animal along with you, what would you choose and how much money do you make?"

First dates are funny because there are always three conversations going on at once: There is the "out loud" conversation and the private conversations going on inside each interviewers head.

"Hmm, he's an excessive chewer. I wonder if I could deal with that for the rest of my life? I do like the way he holds his fork though... Our kids would be good fork holders..."

"Oh man, that joke just totally bombed. I need to recover and say something spiritual or smart... Hey! There's hockey on tonight. Maybe can I sneak away and check the score if I say I'm going to the washroom and detour by a TV... oh shoot, I think she just said something I was supposed to hear..."

Step Four: Defining The Relationship (The "DTR")

Things progress and after a few dates, phone calls, walks, coffee times, etc., there comes a time to address what exactly is going on between the couple: Why do you keep calling me? Why do we keep hanging out together? Where is this relationship going and how long is it going to take to get there?

Girls need DTR's (or "defining the relationship" talks) to know if the guy is just dragging her along, wasting her pretty years or if he really is serious about committing to her. Guys need DTRs to figure out if this is the girl he is serious about committing to. DTRs are effective ways to get both parties on the same page. If a guy does not like a girl, he will avoid the DTR by any means necessary. Author Greg Behrendt author of *He's Just Not That Into You* says that a guy would rather be trampled by a herd of elephants on fire than tell a girl he is not that into her. The girl deserves to hear the truth, and a DTR can provoke both the guy and girl to get their intentions out in the open.

A DTR can end in three ways: 1) Nothing happens, everything stays the same. 2) There will be a mutually agreed upon lie to attempt the impossible, "Let's just be friends," or 3) The relationship progresses into dating, courting, or a mix of the two informally titled, "dourting."

Step Five: The Relationship

Having moved past all the initial cat and mouse chase of "should I call or not?", "tell the truth or lie?" stage, soon enough the couple begins to reveal who they really are. This gives the person you are dating a chance to accept or reject you as a potential lifetime mate. Is that not the greatest risk a person can take? Your heart, the most intimate and vulnerable part of who you are, is opened up to someone you are just getting to know and trust. When dating, you are taking your heart in an open hand and passing it off to another person essentially saying,

"Here, do what you want with this."

Sometimes the recipient will take it and trample it; sometimes it will be taken and cherished.

Finding the latter often takes a few experiences with the former, and that is why we call it "heartbreaking" when a relationship does not work out. It hurts a lot to be broken — broken things need to be healed before they can be whole again. The most fragile of things in the world often take the longest to heal. This is why Proverbs says, "Above all else, guard your heart, for it is the wellspring of life[97]."

This whole process is a lot of work — from the awkward walk across the room while trying not to make a fool of yourself to the phone calls, first dates, and vulnerability of just being yourself, willing to get hurt.

So why do we bother going through with all this? Why do we bother with opposite sex relationships when there is so much work and risk involved?

It's A Good, God Thing

We put up with so much because the end result is worth it. Humans all throughout history have been intrigued by the idea of love and have always had the desire to be in it. It is a beautiful gift to share committed romantic love with another person, and that's why we do it so often. That's why people write songs, poems, and movies about love. This is why there are always weddings going on. It's a good thing; yes, it's a God thing.

Our desire to love someone and be loved in return comes from God. He put it there. The Bible starts with a wedding with

---

[97]   Proverbs 4:23

Adam and Eve, and it ends with a wedding in the final chapter of Revelation as Jesus unites with His Church.

The first wedding occurs after the creation of the world. Following each day of creation, God proclaimed that everything was good, but in the case of humanity on the sixth day, He went one step further and called us humans, "very good."

With all God's creating and proclaiming in those early days, there was one thing in creation that God called "not good." It was not good for a man, in this case Adam, to be all by himself[98]. It was not fatal for Adam to be alone, it was just "not good."

Have you ever heard that little sermon that married people love to preach to you about how "As soon as you're happy being single and not looking for anyone, that's when the right person comes along?" Well don't believe them. They are lying to you.

It gets ridiculous when some try to live out this kind of talk. All you get is a bunch of people pretending that they don't really want or need anyone while secretly hoping they are saying the right thing so that the "right person" will come quicker.

So you have girls who are told, "As soon as you don't care about guys, that's when God brings a guy around." The girl, who is excited for the day Mr. Right comes along, hears that and says, "Okay, I don't care about guys…" and then she waits… but no one comes so she says it a little louder this time. "Ahem! I said, 'I don't need a guy around!'" This is self-deception of course.

It's not just girls who deceive themselves. It happens to guys too. Guys hear stuff like, "Just wait around and, at the right time, God will bring the right girl right to you." So the guy is to sit there and wait for something to happen… but do guys treat anything else in life like this?

---

[98]   Genesis 2:18

"Hmm, I'm hungry. I'm going to sit around and wait for some food to come." No.

"I'm thirsty. I hope a glass of water shows up right now... I'm just going to wait here until it does..."

It's all a big lie. You are not supposed to be totally fine on your own; it is okay that you want to be in a serious, committed relationship one day. At no time was any married person perfectly happy before they met their future spouse or else they *wouldn't have bothered meeting them in the first place.* If they were content as they were, I always ask, why would they have bothered with the whole meeting, phoning, DTRing, dating, engagement and marriage process? It's expensive, time consuming, emotionally taxing, and what's the point if you've already got everything you want when it's just... you?

God made us to desire and even need relationship with the opposite sex.

If nothing else, it promotes the continuation of the human race.

The First Wedding

Here's how the first recorded wedding went in the Bible. After God called Adam lonely on his own, He put Adam into a deep sleep and mysteriously made Eve out of a rib from his side. He brings Eve, the pinnacle of creation, to Adam in Genesis 2:22.

Adam and Eve are joined together by God — the first wedding. In the Bible, when two people become married, they become "one flesh[99]." That's what happens when a man and woman pair up; the formerly two individuals now become just the one. As C.S. Lewis writes, "The inventor of the human machine was

---

[99]   Genesis 2:24

telling us that its two halves; the male and the female were made to be combined together in pairs[100]."

Adam brought his God-given masculinity to Eve. Eve brought her God-given femininity to Adam. They complemented each other as God made them to do. They were naked and not ashamed of who they were. They shared their life together. They hung out with God together. They were one.

Then sin came and messed up everything.

Divorce is a tragedy — two people come together harmoniously as one body in marriage, and all of a sudden they split up and try to make two again. If you have ever glued two pieces of construction paper together, let them dry and then tried to take them apart again, you will know that they can never be as they were originally.

And The Weddings Keep Coming

Ever since that very first wedding, God has been bringing sons of Adam and daughters of Eve together as one. Guys have been marrying girls because they are pretty, soft and smell nice. Girls marry guys because we're… um… I guess because we are different from girls and can help keep them warm.

So far we have established that the desire you have inside of you to share your life with someone comes from God, and at the right time, you will most likely get married. Before you enjoy spending the rest of your life married to someone, there is another great gift that you can enjoy right away:

Being single.

---

[100] Lewis, C.S. *Mere Christianity.* (HarperCollins, 1952) Page 104.

"But what if I end up as a lonely spinster with blue hair and thirty-six cats?" It might happen and I give no guarantees you won't end up with a lot of cats other than offering this one statistic about how 93% of people will get married at some point. I don't even have a good source for it, but it sounds right to me. I think that the vast majority of people who want to be married, end up married.

So if marriage is on your "eventual radar," it should most likely happen and that is a great thing to desire.

The point of this chapter then is only to pose this one question,

Until that day, what is your hurry?

Desires Gone Wild

The next couple of paragraphs will talk about what happens when those natural desires for intimacy with the opposite sex go wrong. When they mix with sin and culture, we start to pursue relationships for all the wrong reasons.

A Few Words For The Girls

Girls, I don't claim to understand you but I have observed that you are hyper-relational beings and that you were created to thrive in your relationships. Like gas in a car, relationships can be your fuel. God made you for relationships with guys and girls. You love connection and desire intimacy. You love talking about people in relationships, even if it means talking so loudly about *all* your relationships that it disturbs all the people in the coffee shop sitting next to you who are keeping peacefully to themselves trying to write chapters on relationships... but I digress.

I'm okay with that — not the talking obnoxiously part, but the talking about relationships part. What I do not like is when I hear girls talk about their need to be in a romantic relationship *all the time* to find value or worth. Some girls have believed the lie that if they "just had a boyfriend," then life's problems would disappear and they would finally be able to graduate from the proletariat "single" class of women to the bourgeoisie, "in a relationship," class of women.

That's God's gift of your desire for relationship gone very wrong.

Perhaps this is just my own experience but, as a guy, I have noticed that I have caused a lot more problems in relationships than I have actually solved. If there is a girl out there who is dreaming of the day that I show up and *solve* all her problems, she is in for one disappointment after another. Some of my guy friends can be found in the same class of bozo as I am in. I know that does not sound very romantic coming from a guy, but it does sound true.

I would hate to see you constantly disappointed because you found out the hard way that a man you thought would be your personal savior turns out to be an imperfect, selfish creature just like you... except he sometimes leaves the toilet seat up and in that way he is different from you.

Girls, just relax a bit. It is good to want to be in a relationship, and one day the right guy will come along. Don't settle for any jerk who treats you like dirt just because it's nice to have someone around.

You deserve better. You deserve God's best.

Before we go on, let me talk to my brothers for a second.

A Few Words For The Guys

I'm a guy and I've hung around guys long enough to know that we really like women. Guys will do a lot of stuff they do not

149

want to do simply because it might attract women. This is why we practice guitar, brag about our sports careers, work out, drive nice cars, put on cologne, wear clothes other than sweat pants, and make fools of ourselves in public… it's all to attract women.

We love the thrill of meeting women, the exploration of who they are, the thrill of the chase, and the chance to discover something foreign. We work hard at this and devote many hours to making our product more marketable to women.

This is why once a guy has found a girl and has her locked in with a ring, he gets fat. It seems like it's part of the deal, and I can understand why the guy could use a little rest; he did a lot of work being on his best behaviour, keeping up a standard of athleticism, getting the right car, keeping it clean, impressing her with the right stuff, and paying for dates. After all that work, a guy could use a rest for a few years. Plus, there are the various bodily gases which were suppressed during the whole dating process they need to be released, and this too is all part of the deal.

Though pursuing women comes naturally to guys, we don't always pursue women for the right reasons. There is something unhealthy about a man's pursuit of a woman when he has bought into the lie that he needs to have a girl on his arm to be seen as important, as justified, as a man. Some guys need to have a girl around to show her off as the latest trophy he won.

"Look what I've got!"

What they're really saying is, "I don't know who I am. Do you think I am okay?"

Now fellas, as a guy myself, I'm familiar with the struggle to understand whether or not you have what it takes to be a man. The people who write the books seem to suggest that the two deepest questions a man asks himself are, "Am I man enough?" and "Do I have what it takes?" Whether you agree with this premise or not, you have to admit that they are in the top three at least second only to "What's for dinner?"

No matter where I go I see guys trying to get other people to answer these "man enough" questions for them. Products of our culture, a fatherless generation, seek to find validation in the Big Three: Money, power and girls. If you can get any of the Three, or better yet, all of them, then our culture says, "Yup, you're a man now." If this was true, one would think that upon acquisition of any of the Big Three, a guy would have the "Am I man enough?" question answered, and could move on to answering other questions like, "How come global warming is making everything so much colder?" But guys do not move on because, as author and speaker Justin Lookadoo suggests about guys who try to use "Sex" as an answer,

> "The more sex a guy has, the more the question shouts 'Am I Man Enough' which drives him searching for more. The man question is never really answered by sex, money or power. It only gets louder[101]."

Men who look to women to answer their "Man Enough" question will never find the answer from her. Men come to a relationship with a girl not to find our answer in her, but to give our masculinity to her. God made us men to come into a relationship with girls from a position of strength, not for validation.

Until you can grasp that, guys, you are not ready to be a leader in a relationship, a marriage, or a family.

Just as guys do not want to be seen as the savior of all a girl's needs, girls don't want to be possessions or trophies, or have to validate their man every couple of hours like a parking ticket.

---

[101] Lookadoo, Justin. *The Dateable Rules.* (Hungry Planet, 2004) Page 20.

Some Advice

We live with this tension: we were made for relationships but will often get into them for horrible reasons. That is not what God intended when he created men and women to come together. Perhaps before we can experience the fullness of God's original plan, there is something deeper that needs to be dealt with in our own hearts so that we may fully give ourselves to another.

That is why I am proposing you devote a few years of your young life to being single. When you don't have to spend all your moments getting to know the person beside you, you can take some time to get to know yourself first. I challenge you to carve out some time to take a good hard look at who you are inside: explore the dark places of your heart, the lonely places; revisit some of the tragedies and events that shaped you thus far so that you can eventually come to the person you will marry with a sense of wholeness, not dependency.

Before you answer the question, "Who is the one for me?" you need to first answer the question, "Who Am I?" At some point we have to look in the mirror and truthfully answer the humbling question, "Who is this person who is wrecking my life all the time?"

I have learned a few lessons during my single years, and think that some of these can be passed on to you. May these suggestions help you during these important, formative years to prepare you for amazingly healthy, God-honouring relationships and hopefully an awesome marriage one day.

Married people tell you that though marriage is the best and most beautiful relationship two people can enjoy, it is also one of the most difficult. Look at the divorce rate; look at the families you know. If it were easy to stay together, everybody would do it. You know marriage is difficult because even Nelson Mandela, who served as South African president from 1994–1999, got divorced. The guy endured 27 years of prison, persevered through horrific, dehumanizing conditions in South Africa and after being released, he spent 6 months with his wife and eventually broke.

"I can't take this anymore!!!"

Nobody ever wants to end up divorced. On their wedding day no one stares across the altar at their beloved and vows, "I promise to start our marriage off well, but then I'm most likely going to get bored of this relationship, and possibly have an affair that will leave me broke, you heartbroken, and the kids forever wounded. My poor decisions will result in a deep guilt and hurt that may continue on through several generations. Oh yeah... I do."

Today is the day to start preparing for the most sacred and intimate relationship that you will be a part of should this be in God's plan for you. Until you say, "I do," you can save yourself a lot of pain by getting a few things in order in your own life.

Getting The Most Out Of Your Single Years

Figure out who the Bible says you are.

Do this first. It is crucial. You have to know who you are before you can offer anything to another person. You need to know Genesis 1:27 which states that human beings are created in God's image. That means that we all have great value that comes from God — a value that no one can take away from you or add to. If you are a human, you have great worth.

"But I don't feel like I'm worth anything."

It doesn't matter how you feel — feelings don't change the truth. I may *feel* like the water in the ocean is not wet, but that doesn't change the fact that if I jump in, I'm going to have to change my pants. I'm not sure if that's the best analogy, but it's all I have to work with for now.

St. Augustine said, "If, thinking of your frailty, you hold yourself cheap, value yourself by the price that was paid for you." What he is saying here is that, should your emotions or experience argue against the fact that you are of great worth to God, you need only to look to the cross and see that Jesus paid with His own life to restore you to a right relationship with God. Your life is so valuable to Jesus that He came from all the comforts of heaven, experienced the limitations of being human, and suffered to the point of death on a cross *for you*. That says to me that your life is very valuable to Him.

When you understand that your value comes from God, and not your relationship status:

You won't need to have a girl around to feel like you are important.
You can be "the only one without a date" on a Friday night.
You can attend a friend's wedding and not pout the whole time about when your Prince Charming will show up.
You can enjoy the gift of today.

Your identity is found in who God says you are and nothing can change that. Until you receive this as truth and apply it to your life, you are not ready to be in a relationship. You will be a leech. Leeches suck the life from people — they do not give it.

Travel

A great way to find out who you really are is to go and be alone for a while. One of the best things I did was to take a trip to Costa Rica by myself. I went there on a last minute flight; I didn't know any Spanish, where I would stay when I landed or what I would do once I got there. You find out a lot about yourself when you're in a foreign airport with taxi drivers of all shapes and sizes yelling things at you in a language you don't understand.

I always encourage guys to get out of the country into a foreign culture and spend some time alone. Throughout the centuries, other cultures have had certain rites of passage that initiate a boy into manhood. In the movie 300, a Spartan boy became a man by going out in the wilderness and not returning until he had killed a wolf. Though a fictional story, something resonates about that story with us. Though we do not really have an equivalent in North American culture today, travelling alone might be the next best thing. I wouldn't necessarily encourage girls to go out and travel by themselves but having said that, I have met a lot of girls who are brave (or silly) enough to travel alone. So who am I to limit travelling alone to just guys?

If you can't travel for whatever reason, learn to get away. I love how the Bible tells us that Jesus would often get away to "lonely places[102]," away from the city, the noise, and the crowds so that He could be alone with His Father.

It is in solitude that we can be still long enough to hear our thoughts.
In solitude we can find out what lies we are internalizing.
In solitude we can find out what we are trying to define ourselves with.
In solitude we truly find out who we are and what we're about.
In solitude we let God tell us who we are so we don't have to let others define us.

Invest In Your Friendships

Friendships are great. But let's just get this one thing clear right off the bat: Guy-girl friendships will always be messy. Just accept it. If you're friends with someone of the opposite sex,

---

[102] One example is Luke 5:16

you might as well stop denying the fact that one of you, at some point, is going to develop romantic feelings for the other and will want to take the relationship to the next level. Either you will get married to them or things will be awkward. That's okay.

If you are a guy, you can learn a lot about girls from your female friends and they can learn a lot from you. They can save you from making a lot of mistakes, and save your future spouse from a lot of heartache. Use these next few years as a classroom to study what works and what doesn't work with your friends of the opposite sex.

It would be good to get another thing clear in this area as well. If you are the type that claims to have a "best friend" who is not of the same gender as you, once you do find your actual "soul-mate," it is time to say farewell to this "best friend." Don't even argue with me on this one because you're not going to win.

I don't even want to bother with a paragraph on this topic, but I will, just because I have debated with enough confused people with the argument that it's okay for a guy to have a girl who is a best friend and another as a wife. It's not okay. Your spouse is your new confidant, the one that you tell everything to. Here's the "knock it out of the park/end of story/don't even talk to me anymore" point I always make. Let's say the situation is unsettled at home — you and your spouse just had a fight and you need a "best friend" to talk about it with. You go to your opposite sex best friend and they are sooooo understanding, very sweet and take your side every time. They understand what your spouse does not. They seem to care more than the person you are married to. They're making you laugh when you're spouse is making you angry.

Who is looking more attractive now? Who would you rather be with?

This is a time bomb. Don't go there. This is why you send a thank you card to all your opposite sex friends once you are married. You thank them for their time and all their help but you must now move on.

Enough about that. Let's get to the friends that really matter now: your pals, your buds, your BFFs.

These people are the ones that you need in your life forever. Learn to invest in these friend's lives and grow deeply with them. Be real. Be open. Be honest. Learn to wrestle together, struggle together, and cry together. I am always very suspicious about guys who can't seem to get along with other guys, or girls who claim that they just love hanging out with guys because "girls are just so catty." Something just isn't right there.

Commit yourself to having great friendships with people of your own gender. Guys, this can get particularly difficult in a hyper-individualistic culture, but it is really important. Be willing to share your life, your struggles, and your secrets with other guys or you will walk a fcvery dark and lonely road. Besides, these are the people who are going to stand up with you at your wedding. If nothing else, you are going to need someone to take the tux back the next day when you are on your honeymoon.

Lastly, though friends may come and go through life's many seasons, your family will be around forever. You didn't get to choose them but they will be around the longest. Make sure your siblings are in your wedding party. Just trust me.

Ignoring that little nugget will make for some awkward Christmas dinners.

Am I The One That "The One" Will Want To Be With?

I read this on a Starbucks cup, "You will only be as happy as the least happy person in your marriage." That's the way I see it too. Are you a miserable person who thinks that getting married is going to make you happy? I don't think it will. Just as fame, money and nicer cars don't make you happy, it doesn't seem like it's any different with marriage.

Were you ever encouraged at camp or at youth group to participate in an exercise called "My Future Husband/Wife Wish List"? You know the one where you list down all of the qualities that you would like to see your future mate possess. I'm not sure where I stand with making these lists to be honest. There are pros and cons to making "The Future Mate List." On the "cons" side, jotting down your "future spouse" order seems a little bit like shopping for a human being which to me is just a little too much of our consumer-driven culture mixed with a brush of idealized romanticism. It is just setting you up for disaster thinking you can order the "Perfect Guy/Girl." You might as well order a leprechaun while you're at it.

On the other hand, making these types of lists goes well with the point I'd like to make in this next section so, for a time, I will support the idea. You should have an idea of what characteristics you would like or not like the person you will marry to have. We all have some sort of criteria in our head anyway and I don't see the harm in putting pen to paper in this matter.

It's good to do this because, as you dream of what you want your spouse to be like, the next plan of action is to make sure that you become the type of person that this dream guy/dream girl of yours is going to want to spend time with... a lot of time with. I will use this example talking to the guys, though it spans both genders of course.

So fellas, do you want to marry a girl who understands culture, understands that pro wrestling is fake, celebrities are plastic and can have an educated conversation with you? If so, you better make sure you can do the same — get your nose in a book, go to school and follow current events.

Do you want a girl who is athletic and in shape? You had best start doing some sit-ups now because chances are she's going to want to be with someone who is in shape as well (round doesn't count as a shape in this case).

Guys, do you want to marry a girl who is madly and passionately in love with Jesus? You better get down on your knees and bury your nose in a Bible because those are the sort of guys that these quality girls tend to go for.

The point is obvious — though opposites may attract when it comes to personality, they never attract when it comes to character. For example, your star football player may by chance fall in love with the band's lead clarinet player, or the straight edge honor student may end up with a rocker chick. That is an attraction based on opposite personalities and will often make for good high school movies. When it comes to character, however, you will never see opposites attract.

You want a quality girl? Become a quality guy.

You want to marry a quality man who loves Jesus and is a strong leader? Become the type of woman that this guy would want to be with for the rest of his life.

You get exactly what you become.

So take these next few years to build some character. Character isn't something that you can get overnight. Santa doesn't bring it under the tree, and it isn't available to download. You gain character by making right decisions at the right times, by gaining wisdom and doing good even when it is difficult or no one is watching.

You build character by enduring difficult seasons in life and remaining true to your convictions, your faith in God, and your unswerving trust that He is always good. You turn to Him, not to drugs, alcohol, relationships, sex, the internet or anything else that would ask you to compromise your integrity and character.

Our character is what sets the path for the types of decisions we will make in life. "A man's character determines his destiny." That was my favorite line from the 2002 Kevin Kline movie, *The Emperors Club*. Paul talks about this concept of "reaping what you sow" in his letter to the Galatian church,

> "Do not be deceived. God cannot be mocked. A man reaps what he sows. The one who sows to please his sinful nature, from that nature will reap destruction; the one who sows to please the Spirit, from the Spirit will reap eternal life[103]."

Ever wonder what makes a bitter old man a bitter old man? It's choosing to be cynical, seeing the world as a glass half empty, and planting thoughts of hopelessness and despair day after day, year after year. My grandma, the most joy-filled, godly woman I know, got that way because she planted trust, faith, and hope throughout her life. She is a beautiful lady today because she chose to live in this light rather than dwell in the darkness.

I turn again to C.S. Lewis for his timeless wisdom on this subject.

> "Every time you make a choice you are turning the central part of you, the part of you that chooses, into something a little different from what it was before. And taking your life as a whole, with all your innumerable choices, all your life long you are slowly turning this central thing either into a heavenly creature or into a hellish creature; either a creature that is in harmony with God and with other creatures, and with itself, or else

---

[103] Galatians 6:7-8

into one that is in a state of war and hatred with God… each of us at one moment is progressing to one side or the other[104]."

I hope you see that this chapter is about much more than just relationships. It is about the type of person you are becoming.

When The Time Is Right, Have At It!

That desire you have to be married or just in a relationship one day is a good thing. It is God's wonderful gift to bring men and women together to compliment each other, and worship God with their "one-ness."

Until that day comes, you have a lot of life to live. There is no hurry. In fact, the hurry that you feel is probably not healthy at all. You may have come into agreement with some of the destructive lies our culture tells. Before you think about marriage, think about living in the truth that while "it is not good for man to be alone," it is not life threatening either. Sometimes it can even be life-giving.

Invest these next years into building character. Do not become a leech — be a giver. Find out who you are and what God wants you to contribute to this world with your life.

And may God bless you one day with a great marriage that honours His great plan from Adam and Eve to the great wedding when Jesus comes back to marry His church.

---

[104] Lewis, C.S. *Mere Christianity,* (HarperCollins, 1952). Page 92.

Suffering Well

What to do when your world falls apart

*"We also rejoice in our sufferings, because we know
that suffering produces perseverance; perseverance,
character; and character, hope."*
Romans 5:3–4

High school graduation is an exciting time in life. It is unlike any other end to any other year that you've experienced thus far. You've got the grad pictures, the goofy robes, the nice clothes for prom, the grad events and the big long ceremony. Grad is a very optimistic time as well. You have a lot of emotion looking ahead to the life that awaits you. Peers give speeches about how the grads of today will change the world of tomorrow, and everyone wants to know what your dreams of the future are. On top of that you may receive encouraging Hallmark cards from relatives that read "All Your Dreams Will Come True."

Back in the day, I really sensed this positive vibe at my own grad ceremony. The class valedictorian read from Dr. Seuss' book, *Oh The Places You Will Go*[105]. Like most twenty-seven years old, I am a big Doctor Seuss fan and would be the first to admit, *Oh The Places You Will Go* was the perfect choice for

---

[105] Geisler, Theodor. *Oh The Places You'll Go* (Random House, 1990)

such an occasion. Inspiring and smile provoking, this story is the perfect story for a grad as it stirs up excitement and wonder about the life that lies ahead. There is one part to Seuss' story, however, that is not so positive and optimistic. This one section seems a little discouraging actually — a part we would all like to skip over. It reads like this,

Wherever you fly, you'll be the best of the best.
Wherever you go, you will top all the rest.
Except when you don't
Because, sometimes, you won't.
I'm sorry to say so
but, sadly, it's true
and hang-ups
can happen to you.
You can get all hung up
in a prickly perch.
And your gang will fly on.
You'll be left in a Lurch.
You'll come down from the Lurch
with an unpleasant bump.
And the chances are, then,
that you'll be in a Slump.
And when you're in a Slump,
you're not in for much fun.
Unslumping yourself
is not easily done.

What's this nonsense about hang-ups and prickly perches, lurches and slumps? What's the deal? Graduation is supposed to be positive and here the always-charming Dr. Seuss has turned into Dr. Downer, spoiling everything with all this negative talk!

And he calls himself a doctor?

So I guess Seuss has to be the one to tell you, with or without a rhyme scheme, that one day your rump might hit a bump and all of a sudden you'll be in a slump. The point that Seuss is making (and I will too very shortly) is that times of difficulty happen to everyone in some way or form; it's natural; it's part of life. Just as much as we all breathe oxygen and eat food to live, we all suffer.

The Bible promises it too. James says, "Consider it pure joy *when* you face trials of many kinds[106]."

Not if, but *when* you face trials.

I'm no Nostradamus and I can't read the stars, but if Dr. Seuss says it and the Bible backs it up, I'm pretty confident that at some point you're going to hit some rough patches on your journey. I'm not sure what it is going to look like because it is different for everyone. Someone might get sick or it could be an unexpected death. Maybe it is a broken relationship in the family or between friends. Maybe it will be a shattered dream you have always hoped would come true or a time of loneliness, a financial crisis, a disability, a crisis of faith or possibly all of the above.

By the way, I'm still debating whether or not it is a coincidence that this chapter comes right after a chapter on relationships. It might just fit perfectly.

A Pilgrim's Lesson From A Pilgrim's Progress

Do you have any books you could read over and over, and discover new insights every time you pick them up? While writing this chapter, I discovered something helpful from a book I have read several times called, *Pilgrim's Progress*[107].

---

[106] James 1:2
[107] Bunyan, John. Pilgrims Progress (Moody Publishing, 2008)

Published in 1678, Pilgrims Progress was written by a man named John Bunyan and has become the second bestselling book of all time (second only to the Bible). In Bunyan's allegorical tale, a man named Christian leaves his hometown, the City of Destruction, to seek relief from a heavy burden he is carrying. This journey he embarks on eventually takes Christian to his final destination, the Celestial City (aka "Heaven"). All pilgrims travelling along the narrow path to the Celestial City must pass through a place called "The Valley Of The Shadow Of Death." Christian has been previously warned that there is no way to avoid this valley, as it is the only way to get to where he is headed. In the darkness and loneliness of the valley, Christian encounters a host of enemies: hobgoblins, satyrs, and dragons of the pit. Christian walks a path bordered by pits of fire, and covered in snares and traps that seek to trip up all who would try to pass through. The pilgrim is deceived by strange voices calling down curses and blasphemies against Christian and Christian's God. It all happens in the pitch dark of night and the pilgrim walks this difficult path alone.

Following Christian's path to the Celestial City, his wife and children come with the help of their guide, Goodheart. Christian's wife Christina, observes the road her husband has traveled and comments on his experience through this arduous stretch of the journey.

> "Now I see what my poor husband went through. I have heard much of this place yet I had no idea it was like this. Poor man! He went through here all alone in the night, and these fiends were busy about him, as if they could tear him to pieces. Many have spoken about it but no one can imagine what the Valley of the Shadow of Death is like until one comes into it himself."

In Pilgrims Progress, the Valley of the Shadow of Death, a reference to a line in David's famous Psalm 23 poem, every character must pass through this dark and difficult part of the journey if they will reach the Celestial City.

Every pilgrim today must also walk through this dark and difficult part of life's journey. As Christina remarks, "No one can imagine what the valley is like until one comes into it himself." I can warn you about what is coming but only you will be the one to walk through it.

Why Now?

Why the valley after graduation? I'm not so sure. If you've been alive for more than a couple of hours, you are already familiar with difficulty and suffering as a regular part of your life. Many teenagers today have suffered far more than I ever did before their eighteenth birthday. For others though, there's just something about those fast approaching late teens and early twenties when things start to get tough. There's a lot of learning to do in these next few years. You're moving out into a world of responsibilities but without the comfort and security of home and the consistent structure of being a high school student. Now you're in the big world and there is a lot that can happen. There will be pressure to walk away from the faith you have had since you were a kid. There will also be tougher temptations, particularly when it comes to your sexuality. The drugs get harder and the parties get wilder. You will have a lot more opportunity to cause great harm to yourself and to others. In any case, you are moving towards your own independence and making your own decisions, and a lot more can happen to you.

Maybe you will do everything right — make all the right decisions — but life just won't work out the way you had imagined or dreamed. Maybe you won't marry when you thought you would or the person you swore was "the one" will break your heart.

Then there are money issues and all the pressures that come from having to support yourself; there are tuition costs, the cost of living, and car payments; there are the cultural luxuries that you have taken for granted — cell phone, Internet, cable, etc. Plus your parents are getting older, your friends are taking more risks, and you're learning to stand on your own two feet which means you fall down a lot. Some lessons you are going to learn the hard way. Needless to say, there will be a lot going on in these next years.

This chapter doesn't sound very inspiring does it? At least I'm telling you the truth. I would love to tell you that once you graduate you will never have to suffer another day in your life. But when your life falls apart, you will chase me out of town because all my wishful thinking was nothing more than that — wishful.

Here are three reasons why you will go through these difficult times after grad:

1. We Need Some Reality

If you have been a Christian during your teenage years, you might have built your foundation of faith in God around a series of emotional highs: you may have attended camp in the summer, a conference or two throughout the year, or a big youth rally that got you all pumped up about your relationship with God. These experiences are great and my life was dramatically changed because of them. They give you big injections of Jesus and people who support your faith surround you. You leave with what some have termed a "Jesus High." That shot of energy, that rush of adrenaline to your faith can last a couple of months, but after awhile it starts to fade. That is until you attend the next conference to get another boost.

The thing is that Jesus is not someone or something you are to "get high on." He is the King of Kings, Lord of Lords, the one who holds the nations as a drop in the bucket. He is to be worshipped, not smoked. He wants us to learn to walk with Him through all experiences of life: the good, the bad, and the times when life just sucks.

Christian mystic St. John of the Cross would say that this coming time of difficulty is a very healthy and most necessary part of your Christian journey. He wrote a classic book called *The Dark Night Of The Soul*[108] which explains how it is in God's nature to withdraw the tangible sense of His presence or put the Christian through a difficult trial to make their faith stronger. Suffering causes people to seek God Himself rather than the gifts that come from serving Him. We move from only looking for the gifts that come from His hand to seeking what comes from searching for His face and His heart.

"Going through this stuff," a paraphrased St. John might say, "is healthy. Just let it happen and you'll come out stronger, more faithful and closer to God than you ever were before. It is all part of God's process for your life."

2. Suffering As A Promise

January 6, 1994 was a funny day in competitive sports history. US Olympic figure skating silver medalist, Nancy Kerrigan, was attacked by some thugs that her competitor Tonya Harding had paid to take her out of competition. Let us not be fooled my friends. Those figures skaters seem so innocent in their pretty dresses and white boots but deep down they can get really nasty too. Cameras caught the aftermath of a wounded Kerrigan on the ground holding her knee and crying out,

"Why me? Why me? Why me?"

---

[108] St. John Of The Cross. *Dark Night Of The Soul* (Kessinger Publishing, 1997)

Over and over she cried out. It was really annoying to watch actually. As annoying as it was, I think this reaction is pretty common for all of us when dealing with life's difficulties. Should something go wrong with us default by crying foul and echo the wounded Kerrigan, "Why me? Why me?"

If you read the Bible, human suffering should not surprise you. In fact, you should come to expect it, especially if you are a Jesus follower. The Bible talks about it all the time. Consider these words of Jesus Himself on what it means to follow Him, "In this world you will have trouble. But take heart! I have overcome the world[109]."

"No servant is greater than his master. If they persecuted me, they will persecute you also[110]." If Jesus went through it, we have to as well.

It was not just Jesus who talked about Christians suffering; the Apostle Paul knew its normalcy as well. In fact, Paul said that he had learned to rejoice when things got difficult because in his suffering, he identified and became more like Jesus. He writes to the Philippian church, "I want to know Christ and the fellowship of sharing in His suffering[111]."

It's all over the last pages of the Bible too. In the book of Revelation, Jesus is depicted as a lamb that is slain and his people "follow the Lamb wherever he goes[112]." If the Lamb suffers, his followers suffer too. If the Lamb dies, they follow in that as well. According to Revelation, Christians will have to suffer more in this life because their lives are in direct conflict with an enemy who hates Jesus and all who associate with Him. So he makes Jesus' people pay for it.

---

[109] John 16:33
[110] John 15:20
[111] Phillipians 3:10
[112] Revelation 14:4

Christians are like tea bags — you don't find out what they're made of until you put them in hot water. It is hard to know where your true allegiance lies until you go through some hot water in your life. That's when you find out what you're made of. So if you're a Christian, the Bible promises that you are going to be led through some hot water. Do you still want in?

Simply put, you are following a man who was homeless, mocked, beaten and eventually murdered. He spent most His life suffering in some capacity even to the point of being called in Isaiah 53:3 "a man of sorrows." We should not think that we are going to get off any better.

I do not know why everyone has to go through all the stuff they do. According to Mark Driscoll's research, there are fifteen kinds of suffering found in the Bible[113]. I cannot do any justice to the complexity that is the human condition of suffering. I have not suffered enough compared to what others must endure. I can only offer a part of my own story, how God has used difficulty in my life to make me more like Jesus and by his grace alone, a leader of His people.

3. Sometimes God Needs To Break Us

In grade 10, two buddies and I decided we needed some help when it came to attracting the fairer sex, and so we made up and laminated ID cards with our pictures on them. We titled it with the bold words "The Stud Club." The inscription on the back read as follows, "These cards are carried by three men considered by many as God's personal gift to women. These studs are well equipped and up to handling every situation that arises. Card bearer is entitled to corny pick up lines and phrases such as "I'm it baby!"

---

[113] Driscoll, Mark. Taken from a blog "15 Kinds Of Suffering" (blog. marshillchurch.org/2009/02/01/15-kinds-of-suffering)

I carried that thing around in my wallet all through my teenage years. Today it is displayed on my fridge as a constant reminder...well I guess of my personal tendency towards acts of stupidity.

I didn't see it at the time but now looking back, I can admit now that I needed a bit of suffering to come my way. Coming out of high school, I was proud and felt like I had all the answers to all the questions even if no one was asking them. Simply put, if God was going to use me like I asked Him to, He would have to change some things in me first.

It was my precious hockey dream that God chose as his instrument of said change. I had wanted so badly to be a star; instead I spent a long time sitting on a bench as a backup goalie watching other guys live out *my* dreams and getting *my* scholarships. That was painful. Looking back, I realize that the best thing for me was to spend all that time riding the pine. God was doing something in my heart during those years that I can't quite explain other than to say he was hard at work breaking that which needed to be broken, softening that which needed to be softened, and molding that which needed to be molded.

C.S. Lewis observed, "God whispers to us in our pleasures, speaks in our conscience, but shouts in our pain. Pain is His megaphone to rouse a deaf world[114]." I mentioned in the introduction of this book that my desire is not to become famous but to make Jesus famous. I could have only learned that important lesson by sitting on a hockey bench for so long. Off the ice, when my teammates were out getting drunk and hooking up with girls, I was in my hotel room being taught character lessons by God as He was teaching me to be the man He desired me to be. I was dramatically changed during this painful time in my life. At the time, I did not know what God was doing. Now, several years later, I see very clearly what He was doing.

---

[114] Lewis, C.S. *The Problem Of Pain*. (HarperCollins, 1940)

As He did with me, so He may do with you. God will bring pain into our lives to bring attention to an area He wants to work on. It will hurt, but we are always better off after going through it. Surgery is never fun when you're being cut open with a knife by a man with a mask. But that masked man is a trained expert and is making you a stronger, healthier human being. God is a skillful surgeon like that. He cuts us open and, although it hurts, it is always for our good. When you're under the knife of the Almighty Surgeon, remember that it is not that God has abandoned you or that He is not good but quite the opposite.

He is, in fact, leading you somewhere.

A Lesson From Moses Just Like That

Moses is one of those characters in the Bible Hall Of Fame that illustrates God's use of suffering to shape us and break us for His greater purposes. It is good to know the stories of these guys because one day you are going to run into them in Heaven and it will be awkward if you know nothing about what they did or why they were in the Bible.

Moses was a great leader who had to change before God could use him. Moses' story is found in the book of Exodus during a time when the Israelites were forced to work making bricks all day in Egypt. Moses spent his early years in Pharaoh's house being told that he was a somebody. He was important, rich, and an adopted member of the Egyptian royal family. Different from all the other somebodys in Egypt, Moses also had another side to him; he was a Hebrew man in a country where all Hebrews worked as slaves. One day Moses witnessed an Egyptian man beating a Hebrew slave, and Moses went to stop the injustice against his Hebrew brother. He stepped in and, in the process, killed the Egyptian. Don't you just hate when that happens?

Word soon got out that the Prince Of Egypt had killed an Egyptian man and a warrant went out for the young Hebrew's arrest. Now a wanted criminal, if he were caught, Moses would be punished by death upon order of Pharaoh. Moses was forced to flee for his life out of Egypt and into the wilderness of Midian, where he would spend the next 40 years herding a bunch of sheep.

The wilderness became the training ground for Moses where God did a deep work in the heart of His soon-to-be great leader. It is in this difficult time of his life where the broken Moses really develops. Totally outside of his comfort zone and the royal riches in Egypt, Moses becomes a shepherd, spending countless days, nights, weeks, months, and years out in the wilderness leading a bunch of sheep around.

There is the once famous Prince of Egypt now out in a field... with sheep.

Just sitting.

Then walking

And hanging out with sheep some more.

Many years later, Moses is hiking up a mountain when he dramatically meets God in a burning bush. God then presents him with a new mission:

"Go and deliver my people out of Egyptian captivity."

Moses responds, "Who am I that I should go to Pharaoh and bring the Israelites out of Egypt?[115]"

Translation: "God, I'm nothing."

---

[115] Exodus 3:11

Moses doesn't think he is the right guy for the job anymore. This shows some interesting insight into how God prepares people before He uses them for great things.

Before God can use you, He must break you. Charles Spurgeon said, "The Lord gets His best soldiers out of the highlands of affliction." It is those who have persevered through the hills and valleys of difficulty that God finds as His best warriors. Great wine got that way because some grapes were squished and then left to sit still there for a while.

Remember when Moses thought *he could* be the one to deliver the Israelites from Egyptian slavery? He thought he could do it all by himself, by his own might. God needed to break off that independent part of Moses so he could learn total dependence on God.

What Moses learned by hanging out with sheep is what I learned sitting on a junior hockey bench.

It was through pain and difficulty that Moses and all God's leaders have learned this truth: We really are all a bunch of nobodies. The good news is that God is in the business of using nobodies to accomplish His work. And not just any nobodies but the one's that *know* that they are nobodies.

For us proud, sinful humans, embracing our nobody-ness doesn't come naturally — it comes with suffering. Paul says,

> "Brothers, think of what you were when you were called. Not many of you were wise by human standards; not many were influential; not many were of noble birth. But God chose the foolish things of the world to shame the wise; God chose the weak things of the world to shame the strong. He chose the lowly things of this world and the despised things and the things that are not, to nullify

the things that are so that no one may boast before him.[116]"

He brings His chosen servants down to nothing so that we will realize our lives are not about us, our talents, or our accomplishments, but about Him alone. God does not want to share His glory with people; we could never handle it anyway. "I will not share my glory with anyone else[117]," He told Isaiah.

Some Inspiration From Some Other Heroes

Still not inspired? How about this: It is this theme of overcoming pain to create strength and character that we have come to appreciate in the early lives of our favorite Bible characters like Abraham, Jacob, Joseph, Moses, David, Ruth, Mary, Paul, Peter and many others. This theme is also used in the lives of our favourite comic book characters.

Take Spiderman for instance. Peter Parker was orphaned after his parents' death and raised by his elderly aunt and uncle. Parker, a teenager living in New York City, grows up being bullied and struggles with rejection, depression and loneliness. He takes a mean radioactive spider bite one day and soon after discovers it has given him superpowers. It is Peter Parker's character developed from years of pain and trial that make him the down-to-earth superhero who uses his powers to help people and stop crime rather than becoming one of the bad guys. We admire the determination to rise above the circumstances, and that is why this story has connected so powerfully with fans.

Another inspiring story of a courageous superhero overcoming early adversity is the famous DC Comic character, Batman. Witnessing his own parents' murder in cold blood while walking through a Gotham City alley, the child Bruce Wayne grows up with a thirst for justice and, training himself both intellectually

---

[116] 1 Corinthians 1:26-29
[117] Isaiah 42:8

and physically, he dons a bat costume and commits the rest of his life to fighting crime as Batman.

One more figure to mention is the story of the iconic hero, Superman. To escape certain destruction on his home planet Krypton, a desperate scientist named Jol-El sends his newborn baby into space on a ship in hopes that he might be able to grow up on another planet. The ship lands on Earth and is discovered by a farming couple that adopts the baby and raises him as Clark Kent. The orphaned Kent grows up with a passion for helping people despite his notoriously crippling, allergic reaction to Kryptonite.

The creators of these three superheroes knew that there was something powerful to a story about a person who overcomes great difficulty early in life to either strengthen his character or redeem the injustice committed against him. As a result he is committed to a life of rescuing others from the pain they experience. They become, in a sense, wounded healers.

So do not be surprised to find a direct correlation between the amount of holy ambition you have — the huge dreams you're pursuing and the burning passion to do great things for God — and the amount of suffering you must go through. As one goes up, it seems, so must the other. This is because before God builds His ministry, He always shapes His minister.

He Always Cares

In the midst of a recent difficult season of life, I was reminded that Jesus Himself knew what it meant to question the goodness of God in difficult times. Jesus' prayer in the Garden of Gethsemane shows that though He is God, He too struggled with the fact that He would have to go through suffering. The night before the most agonizing day any human being would ever have to live through, the eve of his crucifixion, Jesus prayed, "My Father, if it is possible, may this cup be taken from me. Yet not as I will but as you will.[118]"

Jesus was saying, "God, I don't know what is going on right now. I know what I want but I don't think it is going to go my way. I know that you know what is best and so I surrender to whatever you want."

We do not always understand why we have to go through the difficulties that we face, but we do know that we will never suffer alone.

Jesus is a God who knows suffering. He comes close and suffers beside us. During His time on earth, Jesus experienced the same trials we go through. There is a Greek word twice used in the New Testament, *splankzinomai,* meaning a "deep, gut wrenching grief." At the death of Lazarus in John 11, Jesus felt, splankzinomai over the loss of his friend. Our God knows the deep grief one feels when mourning the death of a loved one. He knows other forms of pain too. He was betrayed by a close friend; He knew anger and felt disappointment; He was often misunderstood and faced constant persecution even unto His own death. As mentioned, Isaiah calls Him, "a man of sorrows, familiar with suffering[119]." This is the beauty and intimacy that the Christian God offers. He is a God who, as David says, "is close to the brokenhearted[120]."

Of course you may not feel like God is close. He may even seem very distant at the moment. In pain, our emotions love to take over, and cause us to think and act irrationally. Our emotions may tell us that God is not good, that He doesn't actually care about us, or perhaps that He has abandoned us altogether. These feelings are not true, however true they

---

[118] Matthew 26:42
[119] Isaiah 53:3
[120] Psalm 34:18

may feel in that moment. What is most true of God is what you believed when you were in your right mind — when you were thinking clearly before you got all worked up and emotional. It is funny how we, as humans, are so quick to give up on God and throw away our faith in Him during the times when we are the least rational. Suffering has a way of doing this to even the strongest of saints. If you find your feelings taking over with lies about God's character, fight to keep perspective; trust that God is who He says He is all the time, regardless of what you may be feeling.

When I was in elementary school, one of the most popular book series was the "Where's Waldo" collection. On each page of the books the author would hide a dorky looking, candy-cane-stripe shirted character named Waldo that readers had to find amidst a frenzy of activity. In the early pages, Waldo was usually quite easy to find but as you got further into it, Waldo was much harder to spot. You always knew he was there because you trusted the author, but sometimes it took a little more work to find him.

Sometimes in our lives it is obvious that Jesus is present and right there along with us. Other times it may seem like He is nowhere to be found or is doing a real good job of hiding. In these times, we must trust that the one who said, "I am with you always, even to the ends of the age," really meant it.

God is always there and He is always good.

Dealing With Disappointment

I get disappointed quite easily. Dreaming the impossible to happen and always hoping for the best, life seldom works out in reality as nicely as it does in my head. I have learned that disappointment is a daily part of being caught somewhere between the fall of humanity in Genesis 3 and the redemption of history in Revelation 21. I have a deep longing for something greater than what my present experience on earth can offer. I dream of a paradise where everything always works out "happily ever after," and every Christmas ends with all the Whos singing in a circle, hands clasped and the Grinch carves the Roast Beast. In my experience, it seldom happens, if ever.

Life doesn't work out like it does in the movies. The roast beast is overcooked and the Grinch stays at the top of Mount Crumpet getting grumpier and grumpier.

Disappointment is a common experience shared amongst all of us. Rather than get all depressed about it, we can use our disappointments to help us see that our truest and deepest desires were ultimately given to us to be fulfilled somewhere else.

I wrote in my journal a couple of days ago,

> "The reality of life is that it is full of pain and constant disappointment. It is the constancy of learning to deal with disappointment and learning to get back up each time your ideals are knocked to the ground... It is believing that God is still and always will be good and that there will be a day when the heart's true desires will finally reach their fulfillment. The gift of pain and disappointment is a reminder of heaven's joys that will come to all who refuse to give up. These present difficulties call us to look to somewhere else, another day ahead not yet here where there will be no more pain and the Lord Himself will wipe away every tear from our eyes. I can't wait for that day."

I get the sense that everything, all those questions and doubts I have carried around for so long will start to make sense when I finally get to hang out with Jesus. All the sleepless nights, the unanswered prayers, the times of great joy, and the greater disappointments will all come together and there will be a grand moment of, "Ah ha! Now I see what that was all about... I get it now." Together Jesus and I will be able to look back at my past sufferings and the sufferings of others as "light and momentary troubles[121]."

Lewis sensed this coming joy when he concluded the Narnia series with these final words in his book, *The Last Battle*. As the characters step out of passing Narnia and into Aslan's country, Lewis describes the anticipation of the new world to come,

> "The term is over: the holidays have begun. The dream is ended: this is the morning.' And as He spoke, He no longer looked to them like a lion; but the things that began to happen after that were so great and beautiful that I cannot write them. And for us this is the end of all the stories, and we can most truly say that they all lived happily ever after. But for them it was only the beginning of the real story. All their life in this world and all their adventures in Narnia had only been the cover and the title page: now at least they were beginning Chapter One of the Great Story which no one on earth has read: which goes on for ever: in which every chapter is better than the one before[122]."

Get heaven's perspective. Life is tough for a while, but one day we will realize it was all worth it. And at that point, according to C.S. Lewis, it just gets better all the time.

The Gabby Gingras Story

In April of 2004 NBC News aired a feature on a child named Gabby Gingras who was diagnosed at an early age with an extremely rare disease called Hereditary Sensory Autonomic

---

[121] 2 Corinthians 4:17
[122] Lewis, C.S. *The Last Battle* (HarperCollins, 1956).

Neuropathy Type 5 (HSAN5)[123]. This condition prohibits young Gabby Gingras to feel any sort of pain whatsoever. She suffers from a nerve disorder that prevents pain sensations in the body from reaching her brain. After I stub my toe or cut my finger, HSAN5 does not seem like such a bad thing; that is, unless you are Gabby or Gabby's loved ones.

When Gabby was teething, she chewed her fingers up. She severely injured her eye by constantly poking at it. As a result, in order to prevent her from causing permanent damage to her eyes, Gabby's parent's made their daughter wear swimming goggles all day long. Gabby broke several of her teeth because she constantly chewed all her plastic toys as a toddler. The teeth that didn't break had to be removed by dentists as a result of a bacterial infection in her jaw.

Those who suffer from Gabby's condition do not live long lives. Feeling no pain, Gabby will need constant supervision and the tragic reality is that she will most likely not live past twenty five years of age. If you ask Gabby's parent's, they will tell you that they have only one hope for their precious young daughter-

That she would feel pain.

If you experience any pain in your life, Gabby's parents would consider you fortunate. Pain and suffering are an essential part of the human experience. Though it is never fun to go through, the best news is that God uses this pain to accomplish His great purposes in our life.

How Will You Suffer?

You don't know what it is yet, but you should know by now that something is coming. Difficulty is on its way if it has not already

---

[123] To see the article, check out "*www.msnbc.msn.com/id/4788525*"

arrived. You need to know it is not the end of the world. Pain can actually be very good for you. When times get tough, avoid asking God to change your circumstances. Instead ask how He can be most glorified through it. Then you trust Him. Trust that He will always be there like He says, and that He is good just like He says. When you walk through the valley of death's shadow, when you experience the soul's dark night, when you face trials of many kinds, may you learn to count it all joy knowing that God has trusted you with a difficulty that will help you identify with Jesus and make you more like Him.

Peter gives us a great promise to those reading this who faithfully endure suffering until the very end.

> "And the God of all grace, who called you to his eternal glory in Christ, after you have suffered a little while, will Himself restore you and make you strong, firm and steadfast. To Him be the power for ever and ever. Amen[124]."

After your suffering, may our good God make you

Strong

Firm

Steadfast

For His Glory.

For the character development today and the joys of heaven tomorrow, no matter what happens you can always

Consider it pure joy.

---

[124] 1 Peter 5:10

The Unstoppable Kingdom

Embracing The Mission God Has For You And Everyone Else

"The church exists, in other words, for what we sometimes call "mission": to announce to the world that Jesus is its Lord.[125]
N.T. Wright.

This is the story about how the Houston Meta-4's, an underachieving football team loaded with tremendous potential, got their mojo back.

For most football teams, the huddle was the place to discuss how a team was going to execute the next play. For the Meta-4's, it was a fun place to hang out. The team loved to huddle and never wanted to leave

---

[125] Wright, N.T. *Simply Christian.* (HarperCollins, 2006) p. 204

it. They never put any plays together because that would mean leaving the comfort that they had found in being together all the time. As a result, they were penalized constantly and never

scored any points. If you don't score points, you don't win football games.

When you lose games, you lose fans.

The team became very unpopular in the media. The huddling Meta-4's became a joke in their community. Nobody could understand why all their huddling never resulted in execution of any plays. What was their problem?

With the decline in fans and public image getting even worse, the Meta 4's knew that changes needed to be made. They hired a postmodern consultant who recommended some futuristic new jerseys and a really cool website for the team. Looking really sharp as a team, they huddled together and complimented each other on their stylish new duds.

But those huddles never turned into plays, which never turned into wins.

A little discouraged, the postmodern consultant suggested that perhaps the answer did not come in the fancy future-oriented ideas but may instead be found in the past. The Meta-4's changed their style to a more vintage look, and their huddles became very liturgical and predictable. Some of the team really welcomed the change while others did not. There was arguing in the huddle. Disagreement turned into long drawn out huddle meetings that

resulted in more penalties and still no wins. The fans knew better. They were just as upset as before — maybe even more so.

Finally the Meta-4's fired the postmodern consultant and hired a pastor from the local church! The pastor knew all about breaking out of huddles for he had taken his church from a similar situation of being too focused on meeting together without going and making plays.

The church learned its lesson, one day, when the people began to see their times together as opportunities to strategize about how to help people and make a real impact in their community. They thrived outside of their huddle by working together to clean up the city, helping homeless people, and drilling wells to give people clean water in Africa.

The pastor taught the Meta-4's that the point of the huddle is to receive the plan of attack, execute it and score touchdowns.

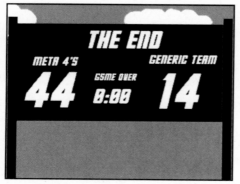

THE END

META 4'S   GENERIC TEAM

44   GSME OVER   14

0:00

The Meta-4's agreed that this sort of thing seemed to make sense, and soon enough the Meta-4's made plays which turned into touchdowns and then wins.

The fans came back and the media reported the Houston Meta-4's were, "The greatest comeback story since the local church!"

THE END

We All Love A Good Mission

Did you ever like to play "Make Believe" as a kid? Sandwiched somewhere between my childhood G.I. Joe phase and the Transformer phase was the spy phase. I remember when my brother and I took on the role of spies who were hired to carry out top-secret espionage missions around our home and the surrounding community. The problem with setting up such an operation in a fairly normal middle class suburban home is that there was not a lot of suspect behaviour going on around us. Mom would be in the kitchen cooking dinner, dad was getting home from work and some neighbours were walking the dog. This was a typical day as a secret agent spy in suburbia. The lack of action didn't matter to us because we had imaginations that could turn a neighbourhood cat into a terrorist plotting to assassinate the president. As top-secret spies, it was our job to monitor the feline assassin's behaviour, and make sure we weren't spotted in the process. These missions were chances for my brother and I to be part of an adventure that made an otherwise mundane childhood day more exciting.

I have since learned that God does not need us role-playing to make life exciting. God has set up a mission for each of us to be a part of. It is a mission for us personally but includes all God's people corporately coming together and then, like the Meta 4's learned, going out and making some world changing plays.

What This World Needs

Having dreamed about traveling to Africa for many years, getting the chance to go in early 2009 was a surreal experience for me. I made some friends there; the more people I met, the more I came to the understanding that, even though people around the world may look different, we are all still very much the same. Humans have the same basic needs no matter where you are in the world: food, water, love, acceptance, hope, purpose, dignity, and grace. We all need the same things, and we all struggle with the same kind of things: selfishness, fear, guilt, greed, worry, and hate. The last group all falls under one big fat, ugly umbrella and it is called "sin." I know of only one worldwide cure for sin.

The hope I have to meet the need in Africa is the same hope I have for North America, Europe, and Asia — it is the hope of the entire world. You guessed it; our favourite Sunday school answer also happens to be the only hope for humanity, Jesus. Only in Jesus can we find the fulfillment of the human heart's longing to be loved unconditionally and accepted with no strings attached. Only in Jesus can we experience life that has purpose and hope, rooted in the promise of eternal life that starts today and continues on forever. Only Jesus can set a person free from the guilt of the past, the burdens of the present and the worries of the future. Only Jesus' finished work on the cross can forgive us of sin and bring reconciliation between humanity and God and humanity with each other.

Jesus is the hope of the world. We need Him to take care of our personal sin but we also need Jesus to reverse the effects of our global sin.

The Church; The Agent Of Hope

Pastor Rick Warren of Saddleback Church in California has identified five destructive issues around the world today that he calls, "Global Giants[126]." According to Warren, these five are issues that we must all work on together to eradicate them around the world. They are, "spiritual emptiness, egocentric leadership, extreme poverty, pandemic disease, and rampant illiteracy[127]." We all agree that something must be done to rid the world of these, but who are the Davids that are supposed to take on such giants of global proportions?

History is the account of people trying one method after another to solve the world's problems on their own. Though well intentioned, it is hard to make a case for the progress of humanity over the centuries when you read the paper, turn on the news, or listen to a conversation in a high school hallway. The United Nations has tried to make peace in our world but they have done nothing to cure the human heart of its tendency towards violent aggression. The government has made laws but they have never made two enemies love each other. Businesses have created economic growth but they have never created true joy. Schools have trained minds but they have not changed hearts. Social agencies take care of our kids but they cannot take care of our sin.

---

[126] See more at *www.rickwarren*.com (March 2009)

[127] This list I have adapted with help from Rick Warren and is by no means exhaustive.

Where governments, non-profits and businesses have failed us, the only group large enough to take on these giants is Jesus in bodily form as His church. If Jesus is the hope of the world, He brings this hope to the world through His church.

Jesus said that He is using His church to establish His kingdom's reign on earth and that this reign is always advancing[128]. What does this mean? It is time for a quick theology lesson.

A Theology Of Church

You will remember that following the first sin of Adam and Eve, God cursed all of His creation. Satan was given a certain amount of power, from God, to carry out his evil purposes on earth. You may recall it is this authority that Satan offered a portion of to Jesus during Christ's temptation in the desert. Satan bargained with Jesus in Matthew 4:8, "All of this I will give you if you bow down and worship me." It was Satan's authority to give to Jesus but it was only his for a limited time. That time was quickly running out.

Jesus came to take God's authority back, and to reverse the curse of sin and death in the world. The way of breaking the curse for Jesus was to go the way of the cross.

I always laugh when I think of the scene from the first episode of season four in the popular TV show, *The Office*. One day the crew at the Dunder Mifflin Paper Company came upon some hard times; more specifically, the quirky boss, Michael Scott, hit a coworker with his car and sent her to hospital with a cracked pelvis. Michael concluded that the reason for the string of unfavourable circumstances was that a curse had come upon the entire office and that curse needed to be broken. Michael wondered out loud what they would do to break it,

---

[128] Matthew 11:12

"Maybe there's some sort of animal that we could make a sacrifice to? Like a giant buffalo, or some sort of monster, like something with the body of a walrus, with the head of a sea lion. Or something with the body of an egret, with the head of a meerkat. Or, just the head of a monkey with the antlers of a reindeer with the body of a porcupine[129]."

This sort of sacrificing, though well intentioned, will not help the particular kind of curse we are dealing with known as "sin." Just before He died on the first Good Friday, Jesus cried out, "It is finished." What had He finished at this point? It was the breaking of sin's curse with His death on the cross. Remember Aslan dying on the Stone Table to appease the Deep Magic of Narnia? It's the same idea.

Paul sums up what exactly Jesus accomplished on the cross in Colossians 2:13–15,

"He forgave us all our sins, having canceled the written code, with its regulations, that was against us and that stood opposed to us; he took it away, nailing it to the cross. And having disarmed the powers and authorities, he made a public spectacle of them, triumphing over them by the cross."

Jesus died for sin, was buried but then pulled the ultimate trump card ever played when He came back to life three days later. Jesus' resurrection was God's final act of triumphing over death and sin forever. The resurrected Jesus then showed Himself to the apostles before giving them their final marching orders. His last words (we now know as "The Great Commission") are found in Matthew 28:17, "All authority has been given to me on heaven and on earth." Read those words again, what is Jesus telling us here? He is teaching that the authority that was once in Satan's grasp has now been restored to its rightful place. The

---

[129] The Office. Season 4, Episode 1. It's a funny one.

powers of darkness, though still prevalent this side of heaven, will be forever disarmed because of Christ's finished work.

After Jesus was done with his quick post-cross theology lesson to the disciples, He then gave them the application to this teaching directly after, "All authority has been given to me...*now go and make disciples...*[130]" Jesus was telling his followers plainly, "I did it fellas. Light has won, darkness has been defeated forever, sin has been paid for and death no longer gets the last word in the world. Now you go out there and make it happen. Tell everyone about what has just happened here."

This was the commission of the first disciples: to go and tell the world what Jesus had done. Two thousand years later our marching orders are still the same; proclaim the light that shines in the darkness.

At the cost of their lives, the disciples did as Jesus ordered and today that light is shining all over the world. Think about it — there are churches literally all over the place. In the biggest cities and in the most remote villages (even before schools and clinics there are churches set up)! The church is the greatest network in the world and here is an example of just how quickly a network can mobilize when it is called upon.

Following Hurricane Katrina in 2006, the relief effort on the Gulf Coast of the United States was enormous. The Red Cross reported that 90 percent of the meals served to those hit by the record setting hurricane were prepared and served by Southern Baptist churches. This means that the churches were able to respond to the crisis faster than the Red Cross or the United States Government. How is that possible? It's because the church is everywhere[131].

---

[130] Matthew 28:18

[131] Again with the help from an article on *www.rickwarren.com* (March 2009)

"You are the light of the world. A city on a hill cannot be hidden[132]." It is our job as a generation to ensure that the light of Jesus continues to shine bright in our churches all over the world. You and I have a part to play as we take the torch that shines so bright and run with it.

There is one issue to address at this point. What do you do when Jesus' church does not always shine like it is supposed to?

A Few Words About Church

As you get older, you are going to start seeing some of the problems with your church or "The Church" in general. You will see inconsistencies with the teachings of Jesus, and the actual practices of the church and church people. With the new freedom you experience as a young adult, there is freedom to choose what you will do about your experience.

As you look around at different churches you may be sad to find that there is no such thing as a perfect church. The reason for this is that churches are full of people, and people are not perfect because of sin. I know that there is sin in my church, because I am a sinner and they let me come in. If they let you through the doors, that's just one more sinner to add to the pile and already we are two for two.

Knowing this, you now have a decision to make: How will you react when you see the problems that people create in your church?

When I was a kid, there were times when I was hurt or did not get my own way. My go-to response was to throw a tantrum and let others know that I was very angry. I was great at throwing

---

[132] Matthew 5:14

pity parties held in my honour[133]. My reaction is a common response among babies. Babies are quick to point out problems and then cry about them. Often one baby will serve as a catalyst for another baby to cry and as the crying babies multiply, there is a lot of awful noise in the room. Imagine with me now if those babies got together and started their own church; oh what a terrible sound they would make together... When I became a man, I realized that crying and throwing bombs at a problem was not the best way to solve it. A man or woman of courage looks at a problem, puts their work boots on, rolls up their sleeves and does everything they can to fix it.

People who complain about church these days are rampant. There are churches springing up all over that grow by attracting these types of dissatisfied, grumpy people. They attract the sons and daughters of Baptists, Pentecostals, Mennonites, Calvinists, Lutherans and Catholics who think that the solution to all their problems will be attending the new church that meets in a theater, has a cool website, observes the ancient church calendar, doesn't read from the Bible and serves fair trade coffee after the service.

A lot of people get dissatisfied with their church, and decide to "church shop" in pursuit of what they hope to be greener, holier pastures. It is usually after six months at a new place when they realize (sometimes it takes until the third or fourth try) that the problems they had in the past seem to have followed them to every church they went to.

I would like to tell you about when I got traded a few times during my hockey playing days for a fitting illustration. Getting traded to a different team is a bittersweet experience. You are bitter that your old team did not want you anymore, but it is sweet that another one did and even gave up something to get you there. With each team I got traded to, I was optimistic about

---

[133] Inspired from a letter written in unchristian. (BakerBooks, 2007). Page 244.

the opportunity to start afresh with a new team in a new city. It was not long after I was given a clean slate that I began to get it dirty again. On my new team I found that I still struggled with the same things I had on the old team. My five hole was still a little weak and my glove hand could still be quicker. I still gave out big rebounds and let in bad goals at times. The new team may have been a new start but I was still the same goalie. My dad was right when he said, "No matter where you go, you have to take you with you." If there is a life lesson to learn about church, here it is — the problems you have with your church now most likely reside inside of you. Changing your location is not going to solve them.

I suggest you start seeing your church as the family that God has put you in. You do not get to swap family members in favour of other more hip, cool or organized families. You grow up in the family you are planted in. Of course, every family has that weird uncle who is just a little awkward and inappropriate along with the weird aunt who can tell you the date when the aliens are coming to rescue her. You just learn to love your family though; you do not move in with the family down the street. Your church family is the group that God brought beside you to carry out His mission of pushing back darkness.

God gives us the gift of community and rightfully so because we need each other. You need to be part of a church family. It is essential. If you are going to grow as a follower of Jesus, you need to do so with a group of people who you can "do life" with. They will be there to challenge you, pray for you, and mentor you; you can babysit their kids and call them up to help you move a couch. A community that does life together is a major component of what the church is.

Bringing The Kingdom

Last chapter I mentioned how your job in the church is being the answer to Jesus' prayer about bringing the kingdom of

God to earth. Kingdom means simply, "the domain ruled by a king." Your church exists to make your city better by letting King Jesus' domain expand into places and hearts where He is not yet honoured as such. To accomplish this enormous job, God uses everyday people like you and I wherever we go. This means that all day, every day, you are playing a part in bringing the Kingdom of God right where you are. This gives everyday life situations *eternal significance.*

When you go to grab a coffee, you are not just getting a coffee; you are bringing the Kingdom of God to that coffee shop and you happen to be picking up a coffee in the process. Remember to tip your baristas... and not just when they are looking.

When you go to work, you are not just working; you are bringing the Kingdom of God right there to your workplace, and bringing Jesus to your coworkers in the way you work, the words you share and how you conduct your life.

How about at school? You're sent on a mission by Jesus to bring heaven's agenda to your school. That will affect the way you study, treat your peers and share your faith. Every day is a chance to get a front row seat to Jesus using your life to push back darkness in your school.

To me, this kind of living is so much more exciting than just going for coffee, getting through another day at work or having to sit through another boring class. Wherever you are, there the Spirit of Jesus is using you to do his work of bringing all creation back into harmony with God.

This is what humanity longs for: to live a life of meaning, significance and purpose. What can be of more significance than being a part of a plan that affects how people will spend eternity? When did you feel the greatest rush as a follower of Jesus? When did you feel the greatest satisfaction knowing that God was using you? Was it not when you were on a mission either during a trip to a poor country, a camp to share Jesus with kids, a trip Downtown to hang out with the homeless, or when you had the opportunity to share your God story to a friend? The excitement you felt then is how we were made to live all the time.

This is why I work so hard to get people off their couches, off their computers, off their video games, and to turn off the TV. It is because there is so much more out there for you! With all the advances in technology and media available to us, you would think that we would be the happiest people ever. But we are not the happiest; we *are* the most bored though. My theory (and it's a very good one) is that things like computers, video games, movies, and iPods were never supposed to satisfy us. They may take up a lot of our time but that's about all they do. Meanwhile, God has an exciting, adventurous life for you and plenty of real human needs that you specifically can help to meet all around the world.

But you just want to beat this level first.

Just make it through this season of your favourite show.

Just want to stay in one more night.

And die just a little more.

Finding God's People In Your City

There is a great passage in the book of Acts where Jesus tells Paul, "Keep on speaking, do not be silent. For I am with you and no one is going to harm you because *I have many people in this city*[134]." It was the role of the apostles to find hearts that Jesus was working on and work hard to introduce those people to Him. It's the same idea today with you. Jesus has people in

---

[134] Acts 18:9. My emphasis.

your city, your family, your work and your school that He wants you to find and lead to Him.

We are all born with built in radar for God. Everyone is spiritual and searching for the meaning of life. Christianity to me has all the answers seeking men and women are craving to experience. The problem is that not everyone discovers these answers in Jesus because of this nasty public image problem we, His people, have. I'm convinced that if the world really got a clear picture of who Jesus is, what He stands for and what He has done for the world, if they met an authentic and fully devoted follower of this Jesus, they could not help but surrender their lives to Him.

But they don't because of this image problem we have. I realized a few years ago that the media does not care about telling the truth, they only want to sell Toyotas. So they pose a debate about a sensitive issue and go looking for a "Christian spokesman" either in the liberal ditch or in the right wing fundamentalist ditch. They seldom go to the normal people because it's the extremist "crazy uncles" in the Christian family who will say stupid things to keep ratings up and shock viewers into watching long enough to see a Toyota commercial. The result is that many of these spiritual viewers (our friends, family and neighbours), though they have some sort of belief in God, conclude that if there is a God, He must not be good. If God is there, He must be a terrible employer for He has too many wing nuts working for Him. In fact, that is a common misconception of God held by people all over the world. I can understand where some of them are coming from because

How could God be good when I'm dying of starvation?

How could God be good if I was born with AIDS?

How could God be good and allow me to be sold as a slave?

How could God be good if I was sexually abused when I was young?

How could God be good if my parents got divorced?

How could God be good if all those wing nuts on TV who talk about God end up in jail or in sex scandals?

How could God be good if _____ (you can fill in the blank with your own)

"God *is* good," says the Christian, "He is *always* good." Though sin and despair are humanity's decisions, rather than punish us for the evil we do to Him and each other, God took that punishment on Himself when He stepped into history and paid the penalty we deserve. "While we were still sinners Christ died for us[135]." Now because of what Jesus has done, "whoever believes in him will not perish but have eternal life[136]." When we were at our worst, Christ gave His best so we could be restored into right relationship with our Creator. It's a great message! It is a message that screams of God's goodness to any who would listen.

Over To You

What if we did not have to worry about what the media said about Jesus or Christianity? What if all of the billion self-proclaimed followers of Jesus just did what they were told to do?

We cannot start blaming all the "other people" for not doing their part because, if we are honest, we are not doing ours very well either. Critiquing everyone else for the church's problems is like punching the air — it's tiring, accomplishes nothing and you look like a moron. You and I can only change the way we are

[135] Romans 5:8
[136] John 3:16

living as Jesus' followers and only influence those we come in contact with. You are the one God has chosen to do the work of reaching the people around you. You are the one who is going to tell the message of the cross, show that He cares deeply and communicate how, through the cross, He has made it painfully clear to the world that He is good.

It used to be that being sent to "the mission field" was about going to places like Africa, China, and South America. The world has changed a lot in the past years. The mission field for you today is right where you call home. Today the people that you are going to run into are dying in their sin and need to hear about the Gospel, the good news of what Jesus has done for sinners. God has people in your city — go and find them[137].

Acts 17:26 says that God Himself "has determined the times set for them and the exact places where they should live." He put you in your city at this time in history with your exact gifts, personality, family, and schooling all to accomplish His purposes of bringing the Kingdom.

You do not need to play "make believe" or live vicariously through Hollywood movies anymore. You have been given a mission of your own: reverse the curse of sin by being God's agent of healing in the world. There is ample adventure ahead in your young life should you choose to accept it. The King is calling. How will you answer?

---

[137] See a great missional passage Romans 10:14-15

The Greatest Question You Will Ever Be Asked

And The Only Answer That Really Matters

"Show me, Oh Lord, my life's end and the number of my days; let me know how fleeting is my life."
Psalm 39:4

The party officially ended in 1514 when a Polish astronomer crashed it. Nicolaus Copernicus was a sixteenth century stargazer who first discovered what is called *heliocentric cosmology*. If you have no idea what this is, do not feel bad; I am only including it because I had to research it for this chapter. Copernicus was the man who broke the news to the world that the inhabitants of planet Earth are not actually the center of the universe. Up until the early sixteenth century, people believed that the planets, stars, moon, and even the sun itself all revolved around the Earth. It was a commonly held belief that humanity, God's most precious creation, was the focal point of the created universe. Copernicus came along with a detailed outline of what was really going on in outer space — planets in our solar system actually revolve around the sun. Copernicus broke the story, yanked humanity off center stage, and thus crashed humanity's little "center of the universe" party.

The Copernican Revolution was difficult for people to hear at the time. His theory was heavily resisted at first by the masses of people (including the church), and if we're honest, we should still admit to having a hard time accepting that Copernicus was right.

I do not like being told that I'm not the center of the universe.

However much I resist his discoveries, heliocentric cosmology is important information to a guy like me. I love to be the center of attention. Growing up, my attitude was always, "Hey is that a stage over there? Is that a microphone? Do you think I could have five minutes?" If you love to perform, have people listen to you, and make your opinions known, then this chapter is for you. Perhaps attention is not your thing but you really want to be rich, famous, influential and do big things with your life. This chapter is for you as well. If you focus a lot on your plans, goals and dreams then, you've guessed it — keep on reading.

It's Not About Me

In 2002 Rick Warren released a book that sold millions of copies called *Purpose Driven Life*[138]. The book struck a sensitive nerve in all of us who live in our present self-centered, consumer culture. It only took one line in the very beginning of the book to have me feeling convicted,

"It's not about you."

I read that and had to pause right away. It was true. I had been exposed. How silly of me to think that I was so important to society when I am just one Canadian guy amongst 23 million other maple leaf flag wavers. I am only one of the Canadians who make up a small percentage of the over six billion inhabitants on planet Earth. The Earth itself is not that significant either I

---

[138] Warren, Rick. *The Purpose Driven Life.* (Zondervan, 2002).

have learned. We were taught in school that Earth is one of 8 planets (not including the rock formerly known as the planet "Pluto") orbiting around an enormous sun which is one of many smaller stars in the universe… and it only gets more depressing the further you go in discovering just how small you really are in the big scheme of things.

God is big. You do not have to be intimidated by that, it should stir up a great sense of reverence and wonder in your heart.

> "He sits enthroned above the circle of the earth, and its people are like grasshoppers. He stretches out the heavens like a canopy, and spreads them out like a tent to live in... "To whom will you compare me? Or who is my equal?" says the Holy One. Lift your eyes and look to the heavens: Who created all these? He who brings out the starry host one by one, and calls them each by name. Because of his great power and mighty strength, not one of them is missing. The mystery of God is that He is the creator of everything and yet He calls us by name[139]."

I cannot help but read a passage like that and get lost in the true grandness of God. Of course, the temptation is to say, "If God is so big, why does He concern Himself with someone as small as me?" To ask these kinds of questions is to miss the point. Psalm 19:1, "The heavens declare the glory of God, the skies proclaim the work of his hands." The greatness of the created world was not made to make us feel significant. It was made for us to see our Creator's significance and get lost in worship.

As John Piper says,

> "The really wonderful moments of joy in this world are not the moments of self-satisfaction, but self-forgetfulness.

---

[139] Isaiah 40: 22-26

Standing on the edge of the Grand Canyon and contemplating your own greatness is pathological[140]."

It would be foolish to stand at the Grand Canyon and contemplate your self esteem. Nobody travels to the Rocky Mountains and asks for a mirror. In the presence of vastness and mystery we are prone to lose ourself in the moment. When we realize the greatness of the One who "holds the nations as a drop in the bucket[141]" we are amazed that He calls us by name.

To look at all of this creation, beauty and say it is all about "God" is to make an accurate statement. In today's pluralistic culture, one need be a little more specific to get a grasp on who God is.

The Message gives us clarity on Colossians 1:16 as follows,

> "For everything, absolutely everything, above and below, visible and invisible, rank after rank after rank of angels — everything got started in him and finds its purpose in him. He was there before any of it came into existence and holds it all together right up to this moment."

If these words about Jesus are true, it would be in our best interest to live our lives according to the truth of Jesus rather than settling for any other worldview that does not see Him as the Bible claims. I believe that the personal and global problems we experience and see around us are due to our failure to honour Jesus for who He is.

"I'm Having Worship Problems"

Do you ever wonder how people manage to screw up their lives so badly? Have you seen someone you love, or even

---

[140] Piper, John. *Don't Waste Your Life* (Crossway, 2003). Page 33.
[141] Isaiah 40:15

just someone you know, make a terrible decision or a string of terrible decisions that creates a mess and causes a lot of pain in their own lives as well as those around them? You witness the whole thing and are left shaking your head wondering,

"What the heck were they thinking?"

How do such messes happen? Nobody ever goes into life thinking, "I'm going to make a terrible decision and really screw up one day." Neither have I heard anyone say, "I hope I get addicted to this stuff. I hope it robs me of joy, money and destroys all my relationships. In the end I hope I get really lonely and depressed."

It is never anyone's intention to screw up their lives and yet, look around you; people are doing it all the time. If it was never our intention to end this way, how does it start?

It is when we fail to align our lives to the centrality of Jesus and place Him as the object of our life's worship that most of our problems start to occur. As A.W. Tozer was known to say, "A high view of God is the answer to thousands of problems, a low view of God is the cause of many."

Greg, The Misguided Worshipper

I want to illustrate this with a story about my friend named Greg that I met while working with the homeless of Vancouver. Greg was down on his luck when I first met him. I could feel the shame that he felt from years of his many bad decisions. A struggling and yet recovering alcoholic, Greg shared with me his life story of once being a "normal young guy" living in Ontario trying to find where he fit in with life and what his life purpose was. Greg dealt with the pain of an absent father that left him with a deep need to be loved which he tried to find in his "party friends."

207

Greg told me he loved to party and he would party very hard during his more youthful days. He felt closest to his friends while drunk and high. Soon the parties were not just on weekends, but they spilled into other days of the week and then there was some drinking to be done *every* night for Greg and his buddies. Greg told me that despite the fun, he still left feeling empty.

Greg explained (and I will never forget this picture) that he hoped to find the meaning of life at the bottom of every empty beer bottle. When he did not find anything at the bottom of one bottle, he would crack another, drink it and look again. And again, and again, and again.

Soon Greg found himself kicked out of his parents' home and boarding a train to Vancouver where he arrived penniless and without a place to stay. He ended up on the Downtown Eastside where the food and shelter was abundant and cheap. It was there that Greg was introduced to harder drugs that were easier to access. He thought he could find meaning in Vancouver, but living like he was, Greg only found despair.

Without the hope or purpose he had been searching for, Greg admitted to being on the brink of committing suicide when I met him. I did my best to counsel Greg, to point him to a detox shelter and to a recovery program. I knew deep down that those things would help his drug and alcohol problem but Greg had a much deeper issue — he had a worship problem.

My friend Greg never wanted this for his life. But who would? His misguided worship came early on in high school and would slowly erode his life. Longing for love, acceptance and purpose, Greg took that God-given need and looked to fill it with created things. He looked to people and was temporarily fulfilled by the camaraderie that came with the party scene.

The problem with people is that people are people and they make poor gods. Imperfect and sinful, they will eventually always let us down. Disappointment with a human being's inability to bring him meaning, Greg turned to beer to fill his longings, but that soon spiraled into an alcohol addiction that he could no longer afford to pay. The addiction had taken over and left him more and more alone and depressed.

At any point during Greg's story, I would have loved for him to tell me that he cried out to God, that he decided to turn to the only one who could truly satisfy the longings of his heart. I know Greg's heavenly Father sat waiting, wanting so badly to fill the void left by his earthly father. Jesus wanted to fill Greg's life with purpose and meaning.

But Greg failed to see Jesus as the reason why we all "live and move and have our being" (Acts 17:28). He failed to worship Jesus and instead worshipped other things. Did they ever deliver?

They never do.

We All Have A Problem

It's not just Greg; it's all of us. We all have worship problems. Sin has screwed up everything by distorting our view of what is important. It has made us think that the pursuit of money, comfort, power, clothing, fame, and sex — things we desire as humans — are the most important things and even worth pursuing with our entire lives. We are tricked into thinking that the pursuit of all these things will make us happy.

This is the difference between being a follower of Jesus, one who acknowledges that Jesus is King, or an idol worshipper, one who makes themselves or other created things their king. The followers of Jesus make daily decisions believing that Jesus is God, while idol worshippers make their decisions as if they were god.

The former worship the Creato*r*, the latter worship the creat*ed*. Worshipping the Creator leaves you fulfilled. Worshipping created things leaves you empty. The former gives life, the latter destroys it. This is the point I've been trying to make the whole time.

That's All Folks

I hope you have enjoyed all these thoughts, stories, and suggestions; I also hope that you have found Truth somewhere along the way. There are several reasons why I wrote this book.

I want you to dare to be different; to live life to the fullest and one day at a time. I want you to see trying to live in the land of Cool as a big waste of time. In a world of grey, I want you to be who God made you to be, full of colour and to offer that colour to brighten up this world.

I want you to know the truth about the ultimate destiny of people who do not know and love Jesus. I don't want you to be a Universalist; I want you to be a Christian. I want you to live the rest of your life knowing that God is truly good in the freedom and forgiveness that He offers repentant sinners because of Jesus' work on the cross. Hell is an awful place to spend eternity. Help as many people as you can find their way to Jesus.

I want you to know the undeserved grace that has been offered to you in Jesus Christ. I want you to find out what you believe and why you believe it. It's not just there to believe in, it's there to change your life. I want you to find out why everyone calls God's grace "Amazing."

I so badly want you to experience Jesus in the face of the hungry, thirsty, lonely, sick, naked, and locked up. I want you to see that you need the poor even more than they need you.

I want you to live your life on the edge of your seat. No wait, I want you to blow the seat up; I want you to be fully engaged in the fight against injustice, poverty, oppression, and slavery in our world. I want you to get your own stories of how God has used your life and your influence to bring "good news to the poor" and how He has used you to change the whole world.

I want you to have lots of great relationships. I want you to have people around you who will help you achieve your life goals. Of course, the most important friend you will choose will be your future spouse. I want you to have character to offer to this person who you will share the rest of your life with. I want you to have a great marriage, where both of you love and honour Jesus with all your hearts. I want your marriage to show the world that it is possible to have one man and one woman under God until death do you part.

I want you to learn to suffer well, to meet Jesus in a powerful way through your difficulties and to be honoured that God would trust you enough to walk with you through the painful trials of life. My hope is that you will emerge stronger, and in your brokenness be used by God in a powerful way to help many people.

I want you to throw your life in with the mission of Jesus. As His follower, you are a missionary to your school, family, friends, church, workplace, city, nation, and to all the corners of the world. There is no limit to what God can do with a life completely devoted to Him. Go and live out the Great Commission — that is our mandate and our joy.

Most importantly, I want you to be able to answer well the single greatest question you will ever be asked, "What did you do with Jesus Christ?" I would hope you now see that your existence here on Earth is not all about you. It needs to be about Jesus; He is the famous One, not you. I hope that you live not to try and steal from His fame but to add to it.

Do you believe what the Bible says about Him being the beginning of all things, the centerpiece of all existence and the end of all things as well? Will you join the song of heaven and all of creation to worship this Jesus as Lord of All? Or will you live like this is all a fairy tale and live like those in the pre-Copernican society, thinking that you are the center of the universe?

God has given you the choice: is it all about you or all about Him? When school is all over, when friends are all gone, when your life's work is done, when your kids are grown up, when all the bills have been paid and your time on earth has been completed, the Bible says that you will stand before God and will have to give an account for your life. For some, this will be an exciting moment. For others, it will be absolutely terrifying. Some will try to make excuses and others are going to be woefully embarrassed. As for you,

What will you do with Jesus Christ?